Praise for *Fight Like a Physicist* . . .

"*Fight Like a Physicist* is a cool co⌐   ⌐   for fans of fighting sports."
—Jeff Fleischer, .

"I have over five decades' exper.   ⌐ual arts but I found myself going, 'Really?' 'Cool!' and 'I didn't   .⌐at' as I devoured this fascinating book.
"Thalken is a fresh voice on the martial arts scene, with an easy-to-understand writing style, fascinating insights, and info you can use now."
—Loren W. Christensen, author, martial artist since 1965,
Masters Hall of Fame inductee

"At a time when all too many martial arts authors pretend to be the font of all wisdom, Thalken refreshingly encourages readers to question, assess, and try things out for themselves. In fact, he outright challenges us to 'break everything,' testing assumptions and limits on our own terms. More importantly, he lays out how to do just that, examining biomechanics, injuries, myths, and martial pseudoscience in depth. Written in an unusually engaging and entertaining manner, this book is packed with invaluable information. I wholeheartedly recommend it for anybody who is serious about martial arts!"
—Lawrence A. Kane, martial artist, best-selling author of
Surviving Armed Assaults

"Martial arts are cool, but martial science is cooler. In *Fight Like a Physicist* Jason Thalken exuberantly unpeels some of the science behind this fun, beautiful, complex, scary, and dangerous thing called fighting. Fun and informative, *Fight Like a Physicist* appeals to both the science and the martial geek in us all."
—Rory Miller, author of *Meditations on Violence*

"The book answers the question of why. Oftentimes fighters look for an answer to justify why we do certain things. Once you understand the physics of the technique the fighter is able to enhance their ability to produce a more desired outcome."
—Michelle Waterson, American mixed martial artist,
former Invicta FC atomweight champion.
Known as the "Karate Hottie."

"Fight Like a Physicist crushes myths and replaces them with unarguable reason. Readers will leave many martial art legends in the past where they belong, with traveling-road-show tonics. Utterly brilliant. Understand more, train smarter, and be smarter than you were yesterday. Get *Fight Like a Physicist: The Incredible Science Behind Martial Arts*."

—Kris Wilder, martial artist, best-selling author of *The Way of Kata*

FIGHT
LIKE A
PHYSICIST

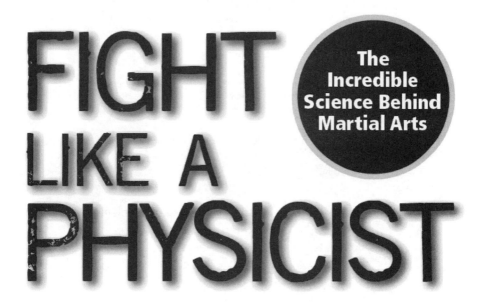

FIGHT LIKE A PHYSICIST

The Incredible Science Behind Martial Arts

JASON THALKEN, PHD

YMAA Publication Center, Inc.
Wolfeboro, NH USA

YMAA Publication Center, Inc.
PO Box 480
Wolfeboro, NH 03894
800669-8892•www .ymaa.com•info@ymaa .com

ISBN: 9781594393389 (print) • ISBN: 9781594393396 (ebook)
This book set in Adobe Garamond and Frutiger

Publisher's Cataloging in Publication

Thalken, Jason.

Fight like a physicist : the incredible science behind martial arts / Jason Thalken. — Wolfeboro, NH USA : YMAA Publication Center, Inc., [2015]

pages : illustrations ; cm.

ISBN: 978-1-59439-338-9 (print) ; 978-1-59439-339-6 (ebook)
"Make physics your advantage in the ring and on the street. See through the illusion of safety provided by gloves and helmets. Reduce traumatic brain injury in contact sports. Give the esoteric side of martial arts a reality check."—Cover.
Includes bibliography and index.
Summary: An in-depth, sometimes whimsical look into the physics behind effective fighting techniques and examining the core principles that make them work: momentum, energy, center of mass, levers and wedges. It also exposes the illusion of safety provided by gloves and helmets, aiding the reader in reducing traumatic brain injury in martial arts, boxing, and other contact sports.—Publisher.

1. Martial arts—Physiological aspects. 2. Physics—Physiological aspects. 3. Sports sciences. 4. Motion—Physiological aspects. 5. Force and energy—Physiological aspects. 6. Mixed martial arts—Physiological aspects. 7. Self-defense—Physiological aspects. 8. Sports—Physiological aspects. 9. Martial arts injuries—Prevention. 10. Hand- to-hand fighting injuries—Prevention. 11. Sports injuries—Prevention. 12. Brain damage—Prevention. 13. Hand—Wounds and injuries—Prevention. I. Title.

GV1101 .T53 2015   2015944822
796.8—dc23   1509

Printed in USA.

TABLE OF CONTENTS

BACK MATTER

Fight Like a Physicist

"A black belt only covers two inches of your ass. You have to cover the rest."

—Royce Gracie

What is physics?

If someone had asked me to define physics during my senior year of high school, I would have confidently answered, "The study of mechanics and electricity." If someone had asked me that same question as an undergraduate, I would have added a few more topics to the list, such as optics or quantum mechanics, but the confidence would be gone. By the time I was doing my own research and working on my dissertation, my answer would have been a very confused and defeated, "I don't even know anymore."

The truth of the matter is physics is better defined by approach than by subject matter. A physicist is someone who uses observation and mathematics to unravel the structure behind this complicated universe, and then uses that understanding to make predictions about how the universe will behave in the future. Physicists will always venture into new areas (martial arts, for instance), but you can spot them by their search for structure, their love of mathematics, and their skeptical-yet-curious approach to learning something new.

When it comes to physics, the universe doesn't care about your degree.

The single most beautiful thing about studying physics and mathematics is that the truth comes from the real world, and not a textbook or a teacher. No matter how well renowned a scientist may be, the truth of his claims comes from testing and verification in the real world, and not from his reputation. Anyone, even an amateur scientist, can make a big discovery, and anyone, including the most famous scientists, can be proven wrong. The point is no degree, no authority, and no social status can ever make a scientist "right." Testable and reproducible results out in the real world hold all the power.

Michael Faraday is an exemplary case of an amateur who found success in the sciences. Faraday was born into a lower-class family in 1791 in London, had only a rudimentary education, and took it upon himself to develop his mind. From the age of fourteen he started an apprenticeship at a bookbinder's shop, and he took full advantage of the situation by reading at every opportunity. When given tickets to attend lectures hosted by renowned chemist Humphry Davy, Faraday took detailed notes and compiled them into a three-hundred-page book he sent to Davy, along with a request for employment. Davy was impressed, and later hired Faraday to work in his lab. Over the course of many years, Faraday's own accomplishments far surpassed those of Humphry Davy. Faraday was the first scientist to draw lines of force describing electric fields, and he built the first electric motor, transformer, and generator. He was one of the most influential scientists of his generation and did it all without any formal education or even an intermediate understanding of mathematics.

On the other side of that coin is a story from the later years of Einstein's career. Albert Einstein had earned his place as one of the most highly esteemed physicists of all time. He is still a household name today, nearly sixty years after his death. He was so well respected that when he wrote an unsolicited letter to Franklin Roosevelt in 1939 about the possibility of the Germans developing an atomic bomb, the president of the United States took Einstein's advice and launched the Manhattan Project to make sure US forces achieved that capability first. Despite having what was possibly the greatest academic reputation of all time, Einstein was strongly opposed to some of the fundamental principles behind the newly emerging field of quantum mechanics. His famous quote, "God does not play dice with the universe," refers to his distaste for the inherent randomness of quantum mechanics, and he took that opposition with him all the way to the grave. In the end it didn't matter what Einstein thought. Quantum mechanics gives us results we can test in the real world. Results that ultimately enabled the development of technologies like the very small transistors in the CPU of your computer or smartphone, scanning tunneling microscopes, and MRI machines. The universe didn't care about Einstein's reputation. He was wrong.

When it comes to martial arts, the ring doesn't care what color your belt is.

Combat sports and self-defense training both share something very special with physics and mathematics: the effectiveness to their techniques and training lies outside in the real world. Anyone can make up a new technique, and even the greatest grandmaster's favorite technique can be found useless. Just as in physics, no authority, no belt, and no status can make a martial artist's techniques effective. Testable and reproducible results hold all the power.

While *vale tudo*, or "no-rules" martial arts matches featuring fighters from different styles have been around for nearly a century in Brazil, something very special happened during the Ultimate Fighting Championship tournament (later renamed UFC 1) in 1993. In addition to selling tickets to watch the tournament live, the promoters made the event available on cable via pay-per-view, and, most importantly, released the footage on video. What they had unknowingly started was a culture of video record keeping for fights, and it would change martial arts forever.

For the entirety of human history before that event, anytime two martial artists fought, either in private or as part of a public exhibition or tournament, each fighter, referee, reporter, and spectator in attendance would leave the event and then embellish, exaggerate, and outright lie about the details of the fight. Whether it was done to protect an ego or to sensationalize a story, the prevalence of these fight lies made it nearly impossible to know what really worked and what did not in a real-life scenario.

The success of UFC 1 led to a continued UFC series, and soon there were multiple televised and recorded vale tudo leagues throughout the United States, Brazil, and Japan. After struggling to gain acceptance for years, the sport of mixed martial arts (MMA) finally took off in the early 2000s, and the UFC's popularity (and paycheck) grew enough to not only attract some of the best fighters from around the world, but also spawn a whole new generation of athletes training specifically for MMA. By this time not only were there more than ten years of recorded and documented fight histories across several different vale tudo circuits, but the UFC's presence was so strong, anyone claiming to have exceptional skill or technique would be obliged to answer the question, "If you're so good, then why aren't you fighting in the UFC right now, or training one of the top fighters?"

Train like a scientist.

Even though it may be possible that anyone can make a new scientific discovery, and anyone can win a fight against a professional fighter, the truth of the matter is the odds are against you. In fact, the odds are so unfavorably stacked against you, if you don't train efficiently and push yourself to the very limits of what the human body and mind can endure, your chances of success are slim at best. While there is nothing new about pushing limits and training hard when it comes to fighting, successful modern fighters are starting to train with skepticism.

I still remember the first day of one of my undergraduate physics classes, when the professor said, "Don't trust me. If you don't question everything I say here in class, if you don't go home and check it yourself because you're skeptical and refuse to take my word for it, then you don't belong here, and you're going to have a hard time making it in physics." I remember it because at first it seemed like the opposite of what a professor should say, but once it sunk in, I realized he was right. Real mastery of physics does not come from memorization and repetition. Real mastery comes from understanding how well the laws of physics hold up when you try your best to break them.

The same thing is true in fighting. You will never really master a choke until you have tried to choke out someone who does not want you to succeed at it. During an actual fight, on the street or in the ring, there is far too much chaos for anyone to succeed just by listening in class and repeating techniques. Everyone needs to have some rough personal failures to learn from. Everyone should have that awkward moment when your opponent's only reaction to your attempted wristlock is a blank stare, and everyone needs to get knocked over once or twice because an opponent kicked right through the perfect block.

Of course, sometimes there are techniques we do not have the luxury of testing out, either because they are too dangerous or the opportunities to use them in sparring may not come very often. You can't learn everything the hard way, but that doesn't mean you can't still be a skeptic. Do you want to know if a spinning hook kick is as deadly as your instructor says it is? Do some searching online and see if you can find anyone who has used it in a professional fight. Chances are, in less than five minutes, not only will you be able to find some videos to watch of your new technique in action, but you will also learn a thing or two your instructor could never have taught you.

The best way to outsmart the greatest minds throughout history is to cheat.

When a physicist makes a significant advancement in his field, not only does he compete against other physicists around the world, but he is often making corrections or refinements to the work of some of the smartest physicists who ever lived. So how does a scientist today stand up in front of an audience and declare that some prior genius's work was wrong or incomplete? He employs every single unfair advantage he can.

A hundred years ago, physicists didn't have computers to solve difficult mathematical equations. They had to do all the tedious calculations by hand, and double-check their work. More than half of their education was spent learning math tricks and approximations. Is it fair to put today's computational physicist and his thousands of computers running in parallel up against the geniuses from years ago with their pens and paper? Absolutely not, but that is how progress works.

If you want to be a great fighter, don't train the same way your grandmaster did. Take every unfair advantage you can and make it work for you. Use the internet and the video records of fights to educate yourself in ways the previous generation of fighters never could. Use a punching bag shaped like a person to fine-tune your targeting skills at home. Incorporate modern technology into your self-defense training, such as super bright LED flashlights. Recent advances in solid-state technology have given us lights strong enough to blind or disorient an opponent but small and light enough to carry in our hands and our pockets. A great fighter's training should advance alongside technology like this, instead of presenting a carbon copy of the tools and methods fighters used to defend themselves years ago.

When I started learning *hapkido*, our grandmaster and a few of his black belts started producing a DVD series with one DVD per belt, explaining the minutiae of each technique in exquisite detail. This allowed students to start learning a whole new way. Since the material had already been introduced to them on DVD, we spent more class time refining and practicing techniques on each other. If students had a question that did not get answered in class, they could review the DVD when they got home. Once a student had done a certain technique a few times in class, watching the DVD was like a mental rehearsal of the moves. As a result, not only did our grandmaster get a strong group of new students, but many of them started advancing though the ranks at half the usual time as well.

When I competed on the University of Texas judo team, my coach had us take a "sparring book" along with us to all our tournaments. After each fight we would take notes, including a fight summary, what we did well, and what we could have done better. The purpose of the sparring book was to reflect on your fights and learn as much as you could. When it comes to fighting, experience is an extremely valuable commodity, and we would be smart to make the most out of every minute. Of course, now that we carry around mobile high-definition recording devices in our pockets, I have updated my sparring book to an online notebook with links to videos of all my fights, and the videos keep me honest and teach me new lessons every time I watch them.

This book was written to be your next unfair advantage. Read it like a skeptic, and test everything you read for yourself. Picture the physics from this book as you train, and remember in the chaos of a fight, understanding will help you out more than memorization.

MATH BOX

Whenever you see these boxes throughout the book, you have the option to skip over them without recourse, or, if you're not afraid of a few equations, you can dive in and learn a thing or two at an even deeper level.

A note for the physicists:

A number of assumptions have been made throughout this book, and a number of technical details have been omitted in order to make the material more accessible to the lay reader. You will find vectors reduced to magnitudes, rotational symmetries assumed at liberty, and nontrivial calculations, such as extracting the velocity of strikes from the frequency, made with little more than a hand-waving discussion. In addition, references to energy and momentum have been given a narrow, macroscopic scope, bounded by the nature of human motion. Despite these simplifications in presentation, the study of physics as it pertains to martial arts is far from trivial, and there are many interesting open questions. I invite you to speculate with me as you read, and I encourage you to contribute by starting an investigation of your own.

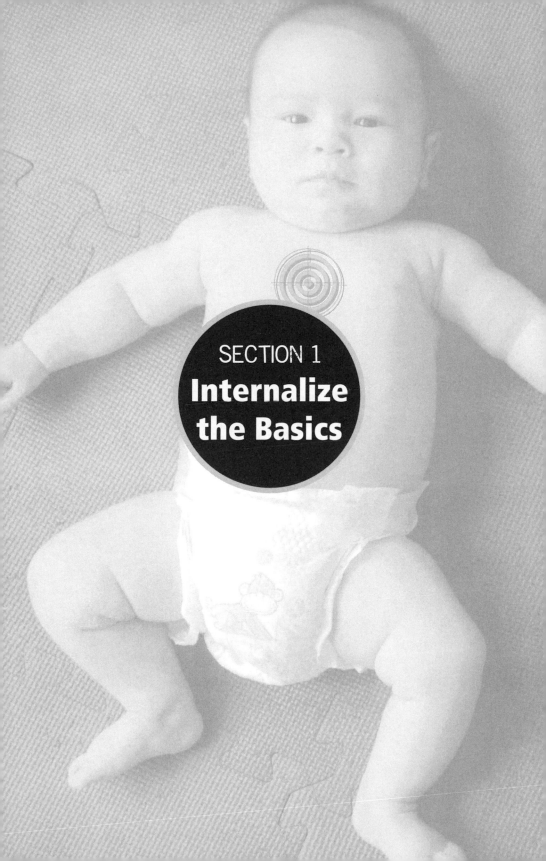

SECTION 1
**Internalize
the Basics**

CHAPTER 1

Your Center of Mass

Where is my center of mass, and why do I care?

Your center of mass is typically located about an inch below your belly button, halfway between your back and your front, and it acts as a central location for all sorts of external forces, like gravity or push kicks. Contrary to popular belief, large breasts (either real or fake) tend to weigh less than two pounds each, and they are not heavy enough to cause a noticeable shift in the center of mass and make a person "top heavy." Muscles, on the other hand, can be very heavy, so professional body builders with extensive muscle mass near the top of their frame may have a higher center of mass by a few inches.

One interesting property of the center of mass is that it tells us where we are balanced. If you want to balance yourself across a horizontal pole like a handrail or a swing, you need to place your center of mass directly over it. The same is true for inanimate objects. If a waiter wants to carry a tray of food in one hand, he

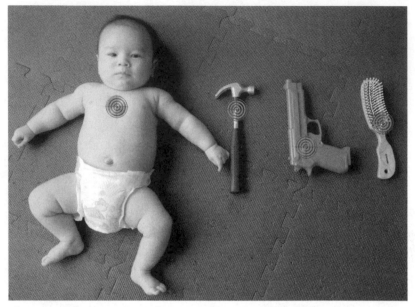

Figure 1-1. The center of mass for some common household objects. Babies are born with their center of mass up in their chest because of their gigantic heads, but it slowly approaches their belly button (where yours is) by the time they start walking.

needs to place his hand underneath the center of mass of the tray and all the food resting on it.

A lesser-known property of the center of mass is that it also determines whether an applied force pushes an object back or rotates it. If you strike or push an object far away from its center of mass, the object will spin. If you strike or push directly into the center of mass, the object will not spin, but it will move in the same direction as the applied force.

In order to put all this together, let's imagine a scenario where you are running around like an idiot, not watching where you are going, when you run right into a fence. If that fence is as tall as your center of mass or taller, it will bring you to a stop. If it had been a high horizontal pole instead of a fence, some of the impact would have rotated your body, creating the clothesline effect we see in slapstick comedies and horrible action movies. If the fence (or pole) had been lower than your center of mass, your body would rotate in the other direction, and you would flip right over the rail. This last scenario, where the fence is shorter than our center of mass, also helps us understand why short railings feel unsafe in high places; if they are shorter than our center of mass, they do very little to keep us on one side.

MATH BOX

The Center of Mass Calculation

The equation for the location of the center of mass of an object is

$$R_{center\ of\ mass} = \frac{\sum_i m_i r_i}{\sum_i m_i}$$

where the summation is over every tiny particle that makes up the object, m_i is the mass of particle i, and r_i is the location of particle i relative to some arbitrary origin.

You might notice this equation is nothing more than the weighted average position of the object, which makes the calculation even easier because weighted averages can be sliced up into any subtotal groups you like. This means if you wanted to calculate your center of mass, you could sum up the mass and location of every atom in your body, or just sum up the limbs, head, and torso. No matter how big or little the parts of your summation are, you will get the same answer in the end.

To find the center of mass, balance it, hang it, or spin it.

If you want to find the center of mass of a person, one of the best ways to do it is to lay the person down on a board, and then balance that board on a stick or dowel. You can then either subtract the center of mass of the board, or just keep scooting things around until the center of mass of the board and the person line

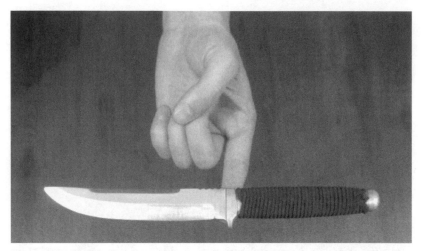

Figure 1-2. Finding the center of mass of a knife by balancing it. Most knives balance right where the blade meets the hilt.

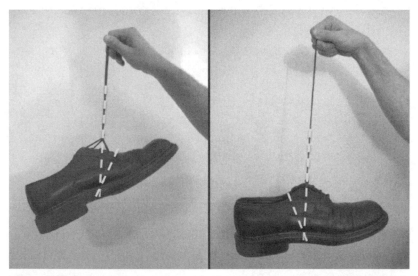

Figure 1-3. Finding the center of mass of a shoe by hanging it from two different spots on the laces. The intersection of the red and blue lines represents the center of mass.

up on top of the stick. For smaller objects such as a phone, a pen, or a banana, you can take a similar approach and balance that object on your finger.

If an object is difficult to balance, your next option is to hang it from a string. No matter where you hang the object from, the center of mass will fall directly below the string you used to suspend it. Usually you will need to hang an object from at least two different spots in order to locate the center of mass.

As a last resort, if you can't balance or hang an object but you need to know where the center of mass is, toss it out a window and give it some spin. As it flies through the air, it will rotate around its center of mass.

Your center of mass moves when you do.

One of the great things about being a human is the ability to move around and change your shape at will. Whenever you bend over or move your arms and legs around, your center of mass moves around too. When you lift your arms over your head, your center of mass rises a few inches. When you bend over at the waist, your center of mass comes forward and down to a point just outside of your body.

When a cowboy rides a bull at a rodeo (or when some drunk dude rides a mechanical bull at a bar), he puts his strong arm up in the air, not because he wants to show off, but because he needs it to stay on top. In order to successfully ride the bull, he has to keep his center of mass directly above the saddle, and even though his arm is only 6 or 7 percent of his total body weight, swinging it around gives him enough control over his center of mass to keep him in the saddle. The hat, however, serves no purpose and is just for showing off.

Just as the cowboy needs to control his center of mass to stay on the bull, you need to control your center of mass to stay on your feet. Anytime your feet are not directly below your center of mass (or straddled across it), you will begin to fall. In most cases, if someone bumps into you or pushes you, you can regain your balance after a sudden flash of panic and a couple of quick steps. Your brain will sometimes panic because you only have a moment to reposition your feet to avoid falling. Your brain does not panic, however, when you shift your center of mass away from your feet on purpose. In fact, when you do it to yourself over and over in a controlled fashion, it is called "walking."

Although your center of mass does need to be above your feet to stay upright, it does not matter if your center of mass is exactly in the center of your stance or if it is closer to one foot than the other. The closer your center of mass is to a given foot, the more weight that foot will bear. If someone's center of mass is in the middle of his feet, each leg will support 50 percent of the weight. If that person's center of mass moves directly over one foot, that foot will support 100 percent of the weight. Any fighter who plans to kick you without falling over will have to shift his center of mass in this way first. It can be very subtle, and nearly instantaneous, depending on the fighter, but if you can learn what these subtle shifts look like, you have an advantage.

Right about now you may be wondering how it is possible to bend over at the waist without falling over if our feet have to be below our center of mass at all times. The answer to this question is simple, even though we tend not to notice it. Whenever we bend over, we stick our butt out behind us to serve as a counterbalance and keep our center of mass over our feet. You can test this two different ways, one being much creepier than the other. The first is to bend over and touch your toes, and then try it again with your heels and butt up against a wall, so you are unable to move and counterbalance yourself. The second is to ask a friend to touch his or her toes in front of you as you watch from the side. Even if you tell your friend it is for science, it will still be creepy.

Your belly button is important for leg sweeps.

Every sweep, throw, or takedown you have ever seen involves either removing a supporting foot (leaving the center of mass far away from the only remaining support) or shifting the center of mass away from the supporting feet in such a way as to make it difficult or impossible to move the feet back under the center of mass.

The fact that we can describe all takedowns so succinctly means we can also boil all of their complexity down to simple concepts. Anytime you practice a sweep, throw, or takedown, ask yourself these two questions:

> *Q1: How are you putting your opponent's center of mass in a position where it is unsupported?*
>
> *Q2: Why is it that your opponent cannot just reposition his feet in time to save himself?*

If you can answer those two questions, you are on your way to developing a deep understanding and mastery of the technique. Alternatively, if you find yourself on the receiving end of a takedown, it would be to your advantage to understand the answers to these questions as well, so you can do your best to keep your opponent from putting you on the floor.

Let's look at a simple example here, so when it comes time for you to answer these questions yourself, you have somewhere to start. The simplest and perhaps most effective takedown we see in the ring today is the wrestler's favorite: get low and shoot the legs. There are, of course, many variations and many subtleties to the technique, but for now, we will stick to the basics.

> *Q1: How are you putting your opponent's center of mass in a position where it is unsupported?*
>
> *A1: Your shoulder is pushing your opponent's center of mass behind and possibly to the side of his supporting feet as you charge in.*

Q2: Why is it that your opponent cannot just reposition his feet in time to save himself?

A2: Getting a hand behind one or both knees will assure you your opponent is not capable of recovery as you advance.

While focusing on these questions will not grant you immediate mastery of the technique, it will get you started thinking like a scientist when it comes to takedowns, and over time, the "magic" behind them will start to seem more and more like common sense.

Sometimes superstition gets it right on accident.

Some martial artists claim your *dan tian*, or your center of "qi" and source of power, is located right below your belly button. These claims are, of course, pseudoscientific garbage, but they represent an earnest attempt by early martial artists to capture the importance of keeping control over your center of mass for both maintaining your balance and transferring momentum to others while striking. It is not uncommon for humans to invent explanations for things they observe but do not yet understand, so if you encounter teachings like these in your training, you can take some solace in the fact that even though the explanations are fictitious, the "dan tian" is actually a scientifically important location in your body.

Advanced concepts: The beast with two backs is difficult to master.

Anytime you grapple—especially if you are competing in a sport with a *gi* or uniform, such as judo, sambo, or Brazilian jiu-jitsu— there is a high probability that both you and your opponent will end up with a firm grip on each other, and together you will start to behave more like one object with four legs than two objects with two legs each. You will have one combined center of mass located somewhere between the two of you, and four feet to provide support for it. In order to throw an opponent in this scenario, you will either have to put his center of mass outside of the supporting feet of this four-legged animal, or you will need to find a way to keep him from using his grip on you for support.

You may find yourself in a position to perform sweeps and reversals on the mat in addition to on your feet. If your opponent is on all fours, you will need to find a way to move his center of mass outside all of his supports. If your opponent is sitting up, you will need to remember he can "post" with one or both arms as an alternative to moving his legs to retain his balance. In either case, it is important to note that when your opponent's legs are drawn into his body, his center of mass will move up from his belly button into the middle of his chest.

Advanced concepts: You are only an "object" when you are rigid.

For most of this chapter, we have assumed people are big solid objects, but anyone who has ever watched a toddler using "noodle legs" in the grocery store while refusing to stand up knows the human body is also capable of behaving like a pile of wet spaghetti. At any moment you can decide if you would like to be one large object or a bunch of little, loosely connected objects, just by flexing or relaxing your muscles.

To test this, hold your hand out in front of you with your arm and your body completely flexed and rigid. Have a friend put his palm up against yours and push you as hard as he can. Chances are you will end up stumbling back a few feet or lying on the floor, depending on how strong your friend is. Now have him push you again, but this time let your arm go flaccid. No matter how hard he pushes, your body will not move.

From time to time a white belt judo student will try to use his strength to his advantage and "stiff-arm" his opponents. This can be an effective tactic to use against other white belts because they cannot get in close enough to try one of their throws, but to an experienced judoka, stiff arms are a gift, complete with wrapping paper and a bow. A rigid frame gives your opponent access to your center of mass from anywhere on your body, so he can throw you without ever stepping in. *Hiza garuma*, or the "knee wheel," is a great throw to use, but there are many effective options available.

The same concept applies to striking arts. When you are rigid, your body will be strong and your strikes will have your weight behind them, but you will also burn energy quickly, and you will give your opponent the ability to control you by manipulating your limbs. When you are loose, what happens far away from your center of mass stays far away from your center of mass.

CHAPTER 2

Energy, Momentum, and the "Hit Points" Myth

In the early 1970s Dave Arneson and Gary Gygax began working together to develop a fantasy role-playing game that would later become the very famous Dungeons and Dragons franchise. They took inspiration from miniature war games played with armies and adapted the rules to apply to an individual character customized by each player. Because the players became attached to their characters, Arneson and Gygax realized instant death was far too dire a consequence for losing a die roll against an opponent. As a solution to this problem, they created "hit points," a number representing the general health of the character, which would diminish with each additional injury until the character eventually died. Today we have video games with incredibly lifelike graphics, extensive online multiplayer participation from around the globe, and sprawling maps with seemingly endless choices for your gameplay experience, but with very few exceptions, we still follow the same "hit point" philosophy laid out by Arneson and Gygax more than forty years ago.

To some degree we all internalize a "hit point" concept when we think about fighting. Fights are too chaotic to plan the purpose and intended outcome of every single punch and kick, so adopting the philosophy of "each punch I land gets me closer to my goal" makes dealing with the uncertainty of a fight more manageable. The problem with thinking in terms of "hit points" comes when we start to ask questions about what makes individual techniques effective, or what it really takes to end a fight.

In real life a punch is a complex and intricate process. At the point of impact, your fist will compress, as will your opponent's body, and depending on the relative speed and rigidity of both you and your opponent at the location of impact, your opponent's body may continue to compress locally, or it may begin to move on either a local or a global scale. Depending on your technique, as well as the resistance provided by your opponent's body, your muscles might apply additional force after the moment of impact. There is a lot going on every time you send your knuckles on a journey, and no single measurement can be taken to determine how many "hit points" a punch will take away. In later chapters we will take some empirical measurements and look into the details of some specific punches, but for now we will skip over all the complications that occur at the moment of impact, and instead we will focus on two separate quantities you transfer to your opponent every time you hit him: momentum and energy. If you can develop an intuitive feeling for what each of these does to your opponent, and you learn how to throw a high-momentum punch versus a high-energy punch, you will give yourself much more control over the outcome of your fights.

Momentum is for knocking people over.

Let's imagine a friend of yours throws his car keys right at your chest. It might hurt, and you might even get a small cut or bruise, but one thing those keys will definitely not do is knock you over

Equation: mv

In English: Mass times velocity

The special part: It has a specific direction assigned to it.

(falling to your knees in pain and weeping like a little girl doesn't count). Alternatively, if that same friend tossed a heavy medicine ball at you without warning, there is a good chance you might end up on your ass, even if you catch it. The big difference between those two scenarios is momentum. The momentum of an object can be thought of as its ability to knock you back when it hits you, and it only depends on two things: how heavy it is (mass), and how fast it is coming at you (velocity). Any other physical property of an object, such as how hard it is or how big it is, has no bearing on momentum.

Mass and velocity are multiplied together to get the magnitude of the momentum, so a large 200-pound man jogging 5 miles per hour (mph) ($200 * 5 = 1000$) and a petite 100-pound woman running 10 mph ($100 * 10 = 1000$) will each hit you with the same momentum and knock you back just as hard. The only difference between mass and velocity when it comes to momentum is that the velocity is what gives momentum its direction. This means if you tackle someone, the direction of the momentum you transfer to your opponent is the same as the direction you were running before the tackle. This may seem like a trivial statement at first, but the directional component of momentum is the key to redirecting and controlling an otherwise unstoppable blow.

A high-momentum strike, or "push" strike, has the ability to move your opponent, or parts of your opponent, and that is an incredibly powerful tool to have in a fight. If your opponent is rigid, light on his feet, or if you strike him near his center of mass, a high-momentum strike can push him back, knock him off balance, push the air out of his lungs, or even send him to the floor if the stars are aligned properly. If your opponent is loose, a high-momentum strike to the hands can move them away from his face and leave him open. Whether he is loose or stiff, a high-momentum strike to the chin can make your opponent's head rotate quickly about the base of his skull, resulting in a knockout.

More momentum means putting more "weight" behind your punches.

If you were to cut off your hand at the wrist and place it on a scale, it would weigh about 1 pound (less than 1 percent of your total body weight), which is not much when you consider you will be using it to knock around a 200-pound man or at least get his 10-pound head spinning. If an average (untrained) person can throw a punch somewhere around the 10–15 mile-per-hour range, this means the total momentum of the punch is 10 pounds mph, or enough to get a 10-pound head moving at an incredibly slow 1 mph. Even if you threw your punches as fast as a professional fighter (somewhere in the 20–25 mph range), you still could not get a human head moving any faster than 2.5 mph. In order to get the kind of momentum you need to knock your opponent out or knock him back, you will need to use more mass than just your fist.

In chapter 1 we discussed how the human body could behave as a loose collection of small parts, or one large rigid object, depending on how relaxed or tight your muscles happen to be at the time. This same principle applies to getting your mass behind your punches, but with a few more eccentricities. The more rigid you are, the more difficult it is to move your muscles fast enough to throw a punch, but that rigidity is also what enables you to put more mass behind the punch. If you can get your timing just right, you can tighten your arm at the moment it becomes extended and continue the motion with your shoulders and hips, giving your punch the mass of your whole arm and even some of your body. Professional fighters can get as much as 10 percent of their body weight behind their punches, which is 10 to 20 times more momentum than throwing a fist by itself.

It can take years of training to get to the point where you can put significant mass behind your punches, but we can get there a little quicker if we apply some of our knowledge of the center of mass from chapter 1. Since your center of mass lies just below your belly button, you will get the most mass behind your punch if you can make a continuous rigid path between your fist and your center of mass. Your rib cage does a good job of keeping your chest area rigid, but your lower abdomen is an entirely different story. Many martial artists yell or exhale (or hiss) while striking because the act of expelling air with the diaphragm provides the rigid path you need to get your mass behind your punches. You will also want to make sure to plant your center of mass firmly in the ground through your legs and hips, not only to include those muscle groups in your punches, but also to ensure your center of mass remains stationary as your punches push into your opponent.

While many martial arts involve push strikes of some kind, no martial art has adopted the high-momentum philosophy more completely than muay Thai. Not only do muay Thai fighters put their weight behind their punches, but they put their weight behind their kicks, knees, and elbows too. Arguably, the strike with the single greatest transfer of momentum from any martial art (without getting a running start first) is the muay Thai forward knee. This strike pushes in a nearly straight-line path from your center of mass along the femur, and it can easily send an unsuspecting person flying back into the ropes or onto his back. If you want to get more of your weight behind your strikes, or add a few high-momentum strikes to your arsenal, muay Thai is a great place to look for inspiration.

High-momentum strikes are incredibly difficult to stop.

In physics, momentum is what is called a "conserved quantity," which means it cannot be created or destroyed without an outside force acting on it. This implies momentum is unaffected by hard plastic or metal plates, or even soft foam padding, because none of those things is an outside force. In order to test this out, take turns with a friend bumping into each other while the other one stands still. Get a good rhythm going, and try to make each bump the same as the last (just enough to make him take a step back is good). Next grab a book, or a cookie sheet or a frying pan, and hold it up over your chest. Did it stop the momentum at all? Try it again with a pillow.

I still remember the first time I ever sparred with an amateur muay Thai fighter, and even though it was years ago, the resulting embarrassment on my part has ensured the memories are still vivid today. At the time I had competed in a few different striking arts (mostly taekwondo and *kenpo*), and I fancied myself prepared for anything. The sparring match was in a ring, after my very first muay Thai class, and I imagined I was about to blow the minds of all of my new training partners with my amazing skills. My opponent was one of the assistant instructors, and he proceeded to push me around the ring as if I were nothing more than an annoyance getting in the way of his shadow boxing. By the time the bell rang, my shirt was heavy with sweat and I struggled to get enough air to tell him "good fight." The problem was, even though I could see his kicks coming and I could put my arm out to block them, they flew right through my blocks and knocked the wind out of me anyway. Fortunately for me, he was a nice guy and he went for my body instead of my head, but I still remember feeling powerless and frustrated that day—in addition to exhausted.

After a few more classes, I picked up on a couple of tricks, and within six months, I was able to hold my own in the ring, even with bigger guys. When a high-momentum strike comes at you, it turns out there are very few available options for defending yourself, and oftentimes they will require your immediate and undivided attention. The first option, as in any art, is to get out of the way or strike preemptively. High-momentum strikes tend to be easier to spot early, and they can sometimes result in over-commitment when the only victim is air, so this is a good choice whenever you can take it. The next option is to put more mass behind your block than the strike has behind it as it comes at you. This means exhaling or yelling to get a rigid path to your center of mass, bracing your arms against your body and your head to make your upper torso one large solid mass, and using both hands to meet an incoming kick or knee. The final option is to meet the blow either before or after the intended point of contact, sabotaging your opponent's timing and greatly reducing the effective mass of the blow. In some scenarios, such as catching a kick to your side, if you step to the right as the kick comes in on your left side, not only do you reduce the effective mass of the kick by grabbing it after the intended moment of contact, but you also reduce the relative velocity of the kick by moving with it.

When you are training with high-momentum strikes (as opposed to fighting in a ring or on the streets), the best way to reduce the momentum transferred to you from an incoming blow is to put as much mass as possible between you and the point of impact. If you have more mass (and yes, technically, just being fat will help you out here), this means it takes more incoming momentum to get you moving at a given velocity. This is why Thai pads for the forearms can weigh four pounds (boxing gloves weigh less than a pound), and Thai kicking shields can weigh 25 pounds. Both of these types of pads feel heavy as you move around and train with them, but neither represents a large percentage of your total body weight, meaning even though blocking high-momentum strikes is difficult, it is not impossible.

Energy is for breaking bones and causing pain.

Let's revisit the example where a friend tosses a set of keys at your chest. Even if your friend throws his keys as hard as he can, they still won't have much momentum because keys are relatively light. Does this mean you should just ignore the incoming keys and go back to reading your book? Even though they will not push you back, those keys could still cause pain and damage to your body, such as a cut or a bruise, in the immediate area of impact. It turns out fast objects with small masses, such as keys or bullets, do not have much momentum—no matter what Hollywood says, a bullet will never knock you over—but they do have a lot of kinetic energy. In the context of a fight, you can think of kinetic energy as the ability to cause local tissue damage in the immediate area of impact. Cuts, bruises, black eyes, bumps, broken bones, and sensations of pain are all direct results of energy transferred to your opponent at the moment of impact.

The equation for kinetic energy may look similar to the equation for momentum, but the little number 2 at the end of the

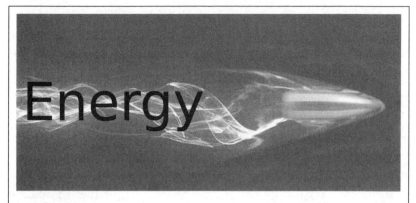

Equation: ½mv²

In English: One half times mass times velocity, times velocity again

The special part: It changes form easily

formula is an important difference. That 2 means we include velocity twice when calculating energy, so mass tends to take a backseat when it comes to the energy of a strike. As an example, if you were able to double the mass of your punch, you would double the energy, but if you doubled the velocity of your punch, you would end up with four times the energy. This velocity favoritism makes it easy to start building a mental picture of the differences between high-momentum strikes, which are "heavy" or "pushing," and high-energy strikes, which are "fast" or "snapping."

Like momentum, energy is a conserved quantity, but energy has the ability to change into many forms, depending on a large number of factors at the point of impact. The energy of your strike can turn into sound energy (thud!), kinetic energy (moving your opponent), or local changes in the structure at the point of impact (compression of tissue, cuts, bruises, broken bones). One important aspect of the energy spent on structural damage is that it is all spent in the area local to the impact. This has some interesting ramifications because it means a strike with a large impact area—from a fist with a boxing glove, for example—may not do very much damage to the surrounding tissue, but if we took all that energy and concentrated it into a tiny area, like the tip of a pen, it would do much more damage to the tissue in that specific area. One extreme example of this surface-area dependence is the cutting edge of a bladed weapon. The surface area on the edge of a sharp blade is so fine, the small amount of energy required to flick your wrist is sufficient to cause significant tissue damage in the immediate location of the edge of the blade.

In addition to causing structural damage, high-energy strikes can also trigger feelings of pain by either compressing the tissue and stimulating special nerve receptors called nociceptors, or by damaging nearby cells, which release a number of different chemicals that can then stimulate the nociceptors. Pain is a difficult outcome to predict, however, because even if you do get the nociceptors to send a signal to the spinal cord or brain, there is no guarantee the result of that stimulus will be prohibitive pain. Oftentimes during a fight, especially if people are cheering and watching, your body starts pumping out endorphins, which will keep you from feeling the full depth of the pain from your injuries until later. Alternatively, if your opponent has been drinking or taking certain drugs, attempts to generate prohibitive feelings of pain may not have much effect on him.

High-energy punches are loose and fast.

In order to get the most energy from your punch, speed is your primary goal. Oftentimes a high-energy punch also involves a snap at the end, where you pull your fist back at the moment of impact. If you are wearing a traditional taekwondo, karate, or *gongfu* uniform, you should hear your sleeve snap with your fist. The snap is a great way to focus on moving quickly, and it also helps make sure your muscles are loose and your movement is fluid, both of which will help you increase your punching speed. While the snap is helpful for developing speed when training, and it is great for making sure nobody grabs your extended limbs, it is important to clarify that the quick return of your fist is not a necessary component of the energy transfer. As an example, the rapid chain punches in *wing chun* are high-energy strikes without the snap you see in other styles, and some advancing vertical-fist punches in wing chun even follow up a high-energy strike with a momentum-generating push from the extended arm.

As a general rule, more mass means less velocity when it comes to throwing fists, so adding mass from a boxing glove or a roll of quarters makes it harder to snap your punches, but there still are some fighters who can get some good snaps going even with the gloves on. This also means throwing a high-energy punch may be more difficult for a heavier fighter.

Another trick you can employ to help get a little more energy into your punches is the additive nature of velocity. Imagine a professional baseball pitcher throws a ball at you at 90 mph while standing in the back of a stationary pickup truck. Now imagine the truck driving at you at 30 mph, while the pitcher throws the same pitch. The resulting velocity of the baseball would be 90 + 30, or 120 mph, which is faster than any human pitcher could throw without a truck. If your arm is the pitcher in this scenario, the truck would be your shoulders, and the velocity of movement for each of them will be added together from your opponent's point of view. In addition, your hips represent a second truck underneath the first one, and if you are taking an advancing step with your punch, your feet represent a third truck underneath the first two. In addition to all this coordinated movement, another method for adding some velocity to your shoulders is to chamber the opposite hand as you punch. This trick is similar in concept to turning a steering wheel with each hand on opposite sides of the wheel, and it is used extensively in *wushu* and traditional karate, although there seems to be little consensus on how high or low that chambered hand should be.

It is easy to disperse or absorb the energy of a punch.

When it comes to defending yourself against a high-energy strike, there are a number of viable options. Evading the attack or striking preemptively are both good options, although moderately difficult ones because of the high speed of the incoming blow, but still possible for an alert fighter. Blocking high-energy strikes can be difficult as well, but the blocks do not require the same mass and rigidity needed to stop a high-momentum strike.

Another option for high-energy strikes is to place something soft or compressible between the incoming blow and the target. This could be something like foam padding, fat, or relaxed muscle, and it works by forcing your opponent to spend the majority of the available energy from the incoming strike on the compression of that material, rather than spending it on damaging the tissue in your body. The amount of foam padding needed to absorb the potential structural damage from an incoming punch, kick, or even a strike with an *eskrima* stick depends on the specific materials and circumstances, but typically a half-inch to an inch thickness is sufficient.

The most effective method for reducing structural damage, however, is to disperse the energy over a larger surface area. Covering an incoming strike in foam is one way to increase the surface area, but covering the target with a rigid surface can be much more effective, assuming the target is large compared to the incoming strike. This is the principle behind the hard plastic helmets used in many professional sports, but in martial arts, in order to protect the fist and feet of the attacker, we tend to use a semirigid foam/cloth/leather combination. Taekwondo-style chest protectors are semirigid, and boxing/muay Thai headgear is particularly rigid just under the eyes, where there is a high potential for structural damage. Eskrima practitioners primarily use sticks and knives for sparring, both of which are high-energy strikes, so their safety gear doesn't have to be safe to punch, and they often incorporate rattan and plastic surfaces, as well as metal face cages.

Every punch is a choice.

Now that you understand some of the subtle differences between energy and momentum, you can start asking yourself more questions as you train. Fighting is a deep process with many dimensions, and it is up to you to decide what you want to accomplish with every punch or kick you throw (hint: it is not lowering your opponent's hit points). You have options, and you should strike according to your own goals. Do you want to cause pain and bleeding and destroy his will to fight, or do you want to knock him back and force the wind out of his lungs? Do you have an opening to land a knockout blow to the chin, or do you have a better shot at a bloody nose? Strikes are tools to get to the final result, and no one tool fits every situation.

It may be tempting to look at a high-energy strike and a high-momentum strike and make a judgment as to which is "better," but they are very different tools. Fight strategy is a personal topic, and the best strategy for you depends on your body type, your personality, your opponent, and the scenario at hand. You may find yourself favoring either momentum or energy, or you may prefer punches that lie somewhere between the two, but as long as you understand these two extremes, you have the ability to make your own choices. If you want to experiment with some punches at home, tape a sheet of notebook paper to a punching bag, a pillow, or a friend. High-momentum strikes will push the target around, but high-energy strikes will make a "snap" sound on the paper and might even put holes in it.

Nobody's punch is like a sledgehammer: Comparing apples to oranges.

Unfortunately, everyone from martial arts masters to doctors to enthusiastic amateurs will tell you something about the "force" of a punch or the "power" of a punch, or which kind of punch is the best. I honestly believe they have good intentions, but if they don't give you the context of the fight and the specific goal of the punch, it's kind of like telling you a hammer is better than a screwdriver without first telling you if you need to use it on screws or nails. When you add sensationalism to naivety in this context, the claims can become nonsensical, and it is up to you as a fighter to separate the facts from the garbage as you learn.

For the sake of sounding impressive, it is common for sensationalist publications to take a single, insufficient measurement of a strike, such as "peak force," and then use that data point to make ridiculous comparisons. Statements along the lines of "That punch had the same force as a sledgehammer," or "That was twice the force required to break a human skull" are usually misleading in several different ways at once, but the most common error you can spot in these cases is the confusion of momentum and energy. If someone measures the "force" of a high-momentum strike, and then tells you the structural damage equivalent of that force (which we know depends on transferred energy and surface area), chances are that person is trying to convince you martial arts are magic, and if you open your wallet today, that magic can be yours too.

As a fighter, you need to know which facts to incorporate into your understanding of fighting and which statements are garbage. If you can internalize some of the basic differences between energy and momentum, and if you can recognize a "hit points" type of statement when you see it, you will be in pretty good shape when it comes to defending your mind from useless propaganda. A good comparison to keep things in perspective is that you can generate a lot of "force" and transfer enough momentum to knock someone over by just pushing on his forehead with your index finger, but you will never stick your finger through his skull. A bullet, with a similar surface area, applied to the same location, could easily break through the skull with only a tiny fraction of the "force" you applied with your finger.

Advanced concepts: Angular momentum vs. linear momentum.

The ability to transform linear momentum (traveling in a straight line) into angular momentum (spinning in a circle like a wheel) is an option I excluded when discussing how to defend a high-momentum strike, partially because it takes us on a tangent into other areas of physics, and partially because it has a tendency to show up in "advanced" techniques with sometimes questionable applicability when performed under stress. Transforming linear momentum into angular momentum means grabbing or controlling a punch thrown at you and changing its direction (without stopping it) to either throw your opponent or get him into a compromising position. Some instructors will teach these techniques as if snatching a punch out of the air is no big deal, but it is an extremely difficult task if your opponent is not a willing participant.

My hapkido grandmaster believed the answer to the difficult task of controlling an opponent's punch was more repetition, so nearly every class I attended would include at least fifty repetitions of our "circular motion" technique, where we would control an incoming punch with both hands and turn the punch around our center of mass, forcing the opponent to bend over. This started from white belt and went all the way through black, but rather than moving on to more advanced techniques, the only thing that changed as we advanced in rank was that our partners became less compliant. By the time I received my black belt, I estimated I had caught more than twenty thousand punches with that single technique, but I would still need a perfect alignment of the stars before even thinking about applying it to someone who had a genuine desire to crumple my nose with his fist.

Advanced concepts: That little extra push generates more momentum.

Even though most of the action occurs as the fist flies though the air, a punch is not necessarily over at the moment of impact. Any strike (even a high-energy punch) comes with the option to follow up the initial impact with additional force generated directly from the muscles. This force can feel like a push or a follow-through, and it generates momentum in addition to the momentum transferred at impact. This push usually involves farther extension of the limbs, pushing off the back foot, or both, and it can be just as important as the impact in a fight scenario.

Advanced concepts: The universe doesn't care who is attacking.

The very first time I ever competed in a martial art was a taekwondo tournament during my sophomore year in high school. I had only a couple of months of martial arts experience under my (white) belt, I weighed in at less than 130 pounds, and I had no idea what I was doing. My first opponent was a white belt from another school who weighed close to two hundred pounds. In my memory he was a giant, but since we were the only two "adult" white belts, the tournament organizers paired us up. The judge gave us specific instructions to go easy and then blew the whistle for us to begin. Without hesitation, I ran and launched into what can only be called a "flying front push kick," which does not exist in the curriculum of any martial art anywhere—for good reason.

At this point I should pause for a moment to mention the universe does not care at all who is the attacker and who is the defender in any given situation. If you generate some momentum or some energy, the universe is not going to say, "Good for you. I will now damage your opponent with it." The universe just takes whatever you generate and spends it in the easiest possible manner. If it is easier to move your opponent back after you punch him with a high-momentum strike, he will move back, but if it is easier to move yourself back after the punch (if he is up against a brick wall), you will push yourself back instead. The same thing goes for energy. If it is easier to compress tissue in your opponent's body, you will, but if it is easier to spend that energy breaking your own hand (if you punch a brick wall), your hand will suffer the damages. This complete indifference from the universe shows up all the time in physics, including Newton's third law of motion, which states every action has an equal and opposite reaction. This indifference means your ability to transfer energy and momentum into your opponent depends on how well grounded you are, as well as how compressible you are.

Now that the indifference of the universe is fresh in our minds, we can continue with my horrible flying front push kick. I leapt into the air, both arms flailing, connected my left foot to his stomach while my leg was still mostly bent, and gave him the strongest push I could generate with my scrawny legs. I have no idea if that kick actually hurt my opponent, or if it even knocked him back at all, but I do know I launched myself backward with that push and my right ankle bucked under me as I landed, resulting in a hairline fracture at the growth plate. The reality of the situation was that I broke my own foot by generating momentum in a situation where my opponent was grounded and I was not, but as a sophomore in high school, I can assure you I told everyone I broke my foot fighting a man twice my size.

MATH BOX

The Force Curve

Force tends to be a relatively complicated and often misleading metric when it comes to measuring the effect of punches and kicks on your opponent, partially because "force" has a strict definition in physics that is often different from the colloquial usage, and partially because the force is a function of time rather than a scalar value. If we want to know the momentum of your opponent, $p_{opponent}$, after impact, we need to know the full force distribution, $F(t)$, over the entire time, t, while your fist is in contact with your opponent:

$$p_{opponent} = \int F(t)\, \partial t$$

where both the peak and the tail of the force distribution can vary depending on both your own punching technique and your opponent's response. A simple force distribution for a punch might look something like this, depending on the particular situation at hand:

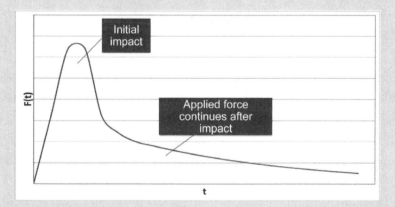

As you study martial arts, you may come across a measurement of the "force" of a strike as a single value rather than a curve. This is almost always a measurement of the force at the peak of the curve, and it is of little value. Not only is the measurement of peak force a direct result of the sample rate of the sensor, but it also penalizes the compressibility of the hand and glove on impact. Using the total force is also an insufficient summary because it requires a sensor time limit and it will favor pushing over punching. The insufficiency of a scalar description is one of the reasons force sensors never caught on in martial arts, despite multiple attempts over the years. In my opinion, when someone gives a colloquial description for the "force" or "power" of a strike, he is talking about many components of the curve all at once, implying both a strong peak and a short but strong tail. The whole process is difficult to keep simple when we talk about forces, so it is usually more meaningful to talk about it in terms of the energy and momentum transferred to your opponent.

CHAPTER 3

The Number Pi and Glancing Blows

The number pi, represented by the Greek symbol π, is defined to be the circumference of a circle (the distance all the way around the outside) divided by the diameter of that circle (the straight-line distance right through the middle). π is a fundamental constant of the universe we live in, with an infinite number of decimal places that never ends or repeats. Somewhere, buried deep within the digits of π, you can find your phone number, your birthday, and any other combination of numbers you can dream up. Even though it is impossible for us to ever know the exact value of π, we can use the first few digits to build an understanding of the relationship between linear and circular motion.

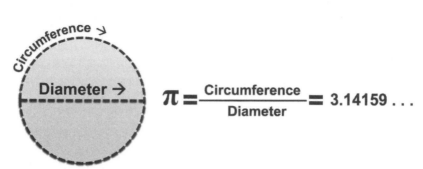

Figure 3-1. Definition of the number pi. Pi is a constant ratio for all circles regardless of size, and it is an irrational number that never repeats and never ends.

A haymaker travels 3.14159 times farther than a jab.

The shortest distance between any two points is a straight line, so it is no surprise to hear that a jab is faster than a classic reach-back-and-swing-around haymaker, but if we want to know just how much faster, we can figure it out using the definition of π.

A jab covers a distance of half a diameter (one radius), while the haymaker covers half a diameter on the reach back, and then half a circumference on the delivery. If the circumference divided by the diameter is π, then half the circumference divided by half the diameter must also be π, so the haymaker punch travels 3.14159 times the distance of the jab. If we include the reach back, this number becomes $\pi + 1$, or 4.14159.

You could throw four straight punches by the time the haymaker finds its way to you, but that assumes your fist and your opponent's fist are both traveling at the same speed. If we consider a more likely scenario where your jab is traveling twice as fast, there are now eight straight punches to one haymaker. This eight-to-one ratio is why most martial artists don't spend very much time training for haymaker defense; it is just too easy for them to waste their time on. This is also why so many martial artists, when sharing stories about applying their skills in real-life situations, start

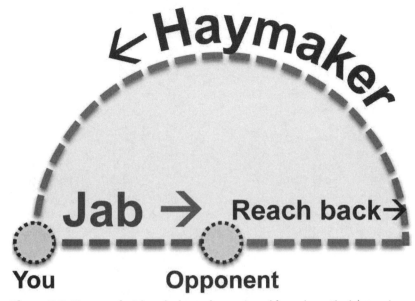

Figure 3-2. Diagram of a jab and a haymaker as viewed from above. The jab travels the distance of one radius, while the haymaker travels the distance of one radius for the reach back, and then half of a circumference for the punch.

off with a description of how amazed they were that such horrible punches really do exist in the wild.

You can use concentric circles to make your opponent run while you walk.

Let's imagine you have an opponent in a standing arm bar, wristlock, or some other compromising position, and you would like to either keep him off balance or make him stumble. In either case you need to keep your opponent moving as fast as possible. One option is to start walking at a brisk pace, forcing your opponent to work hard to keep stride and maintain balance. This is a good option if you have a particular location you need to take your opponent (such as out the front door), but if you don't have a destination in mind, you can make your opponent work much harder by pulling him along a circular path.

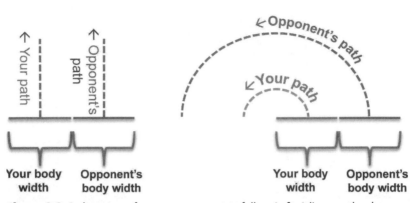

Figure 3-3. Paths you can force your opponent to follow. **Left:** A linear path, where you and your opponent travel the same distance. **Right:** A circular path, where your opponent travels the longer distance along the outer circle and must walk much faster to keep up.

If you can swing your own body around in a tight circle (for simplicity, let's say you just pivot around a single foot), the radius of your circular path would be approximately half the width of your own body, but the radius of your opponent's circular path would be three halves the width of your body, depending on how you are holding him. Since π is a constant for all circles, if the diameter of your opponent's circle is three times the diameter of your own, he will have to move three times as far (and three times as fast) if he wants to stay on his feet. If you want to take full advantage of this effect, next time you have a chance to spin an opponent around, keep him as far away from your center as possible while still maintaining control. In addition, if you ever end up on the outside of one of these circles as your opponent spins you around, try to remember that the tighter in to your opponent you can get, the less work you will have to do to keep your balance.

Here is a fun little experiment you can try at home to see just how difficult it can be to keep up in a scenario like this one. Line up shoulder to shoulder with two friends (you can also do it with just one, but the effects are less dramatic). The person on the left starts off slowly and spins around in a stationary circle, while the person in the middle moves to keep his shoulders in line with the person on the left, and the person on the right moves to keep his shoulders in line as well. For slow rotations it is possible to keep up, but you can already see that the person on the outside is moving much faster. As the person spinning on the left increases to a moderate speed, the job of the person on the outside circle becomes impossible—usually with comical results.

A circular path can protect you from the full force of gravity.

During my years at the University of Texas, I had the good fortune to train and compete with the UT judo team, where the skill and the athleticism of the team and the coaches humbled me on a regular basis. At the time I was still a scrawny kid, so the weight and skill differences resulted in my becoming well acquainted with taking solid throws from bigger guys. In judo, when you perform a well-executed throw (an *ippon*), it means your opponent lands on his back (hopefully with you on top of him), and the impact typically transfers sufficient momentum to push the air right out of his lungs. This can leave the diaphragm temporarily unresponsive, which makes it difficult to breathe, and your opponent is left feeling light headed, exhausted, and disoriented. If your opponent uses proper falling technique, it can help keep him safe from breaking bones or hitting his head, but a solid throw can still end a fight even if your opponent knows how to take a fall.

Many years after my humbling experiences in judo, I once again felt the devastating effects of gravity when I challenged a traditional karate black belt at a mixed martial arts gym in California. My opponent was athletic, confident, and had a calm disposition. He took a low stance and kept his hands at chest level, so I decided early on that my best opportunity would be a kick to the head. The fight started off slow, as we felt each other out, but eventually I hatched a plan to stick my foot in his face. I stared at his front leg (which was vulnerable, given his low stance), turned my hips, and brought my back leg around as though I would kick it out from under him, but then at the last second, I brought my knee up into a sidekick to his face . . . or where his face would have been. Unfortunately for me, he had seen through my bad acting from the beginning, stepped to the side, and swept me with such force he lifted my standing leg up parallel to my kicking leg (which was level with my face). I dropped to the ground flat on my back and had the wind knocked out of me just like getting thrown in judo. My very kind opponent, who had no intention of hurting me, propped me up on my feet, patted my back, and apologized before I even realized what had happened. Out of some combination of curiosity (Is it even possible to keep fighting after that?) and stupidity (Hey, everyone, look how tough I am!), I pushed him off and yelled some nonsense about how the bell hadn't rung so the fight wasn't over. We touched gloves and I stumbled around like a drunk, barely able to keep my hands up for the remainder of the fight, while my opponent took mercy on me and peppered me with gentle taps all over my head and body.

A free fall directly to the ground is a dangerous situation you want to avoid no matter what style you practice. For the purposes of this book, we will not cover individual techniques or strategies for staying on your feet, but we will take a look at the physics behind a direct free fall and compare it to the circular path you take when you tip over with at least one foot planted on the ground.

If a haymaker (half circle) travels π times farther than a jab (half diameter), then your center of mass must travel $\pi/2$ (approximately 1.57) times farther along the quarter-circle "planted foot" path than it would on the direct "free fall" path.

The longer distance may give you more time to think on the way down, but the most important difference between the two paths is the direction you travel. The "free fall" path is in the same

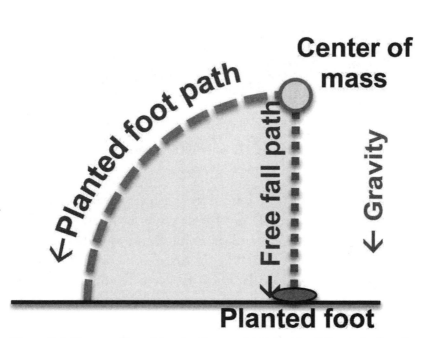

Figure 3-4. Diagram of two different paths you might take when falling to the floor. If you fall without any support, you will take the "free fall" path. If you maintain a rigid planted foot, and tip over, you will take the circular "planted foot" path.

direction as gravity for the entire duration of the fall, but the "planted foot" path starts off moving mostly to the side, and then eventually points down with gravity only at the very end. Forces (like gravity) have a specific direction they push in, so if something rigid (like your leg) makes you move in a direction that is not fully aligned with the force, you will feel only a fraction of that force. The classic example physicists like to use is a ramp.

If the ramp is steep, then the slope of the ramp is closely aligned with gravity, and you will experience rapid acceleration down the ramp. If the ramp is close to horizontal, you will experience only moderate acceleration. Calculating the exact percentage of gravity you feel at a particular angle requires a little bit of trigonometry (the sine of the ramp's angle times free-fall acceleration), but for our purposes here, it is sufficient to know the percentage goes up at steeper angles.

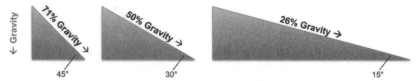

Figure 3-5. The percent of gravitational acceleration realized when sliding down ramps of various angles. Steeper angles result in a larger percentage of gravity. To find the percentage for these examples, take the sine of the angle of the ramp.

Gravity accelerates you toward the earth at a rate of 32 feet per second squared (9.8 m/s²), so if your center of mass (just below your belly button) is 3 feet off the ground, and you fall directly to the floor, you would be falling 14 ft/sec, or about 9.5 mph on impact. In order to calculate how fast you hit the floor on the circular path, we need to break up the circle into a series of tiny ramps, and then sum up the effect of each ramp.

MATH BOX

Calculating the Circular Path Final Velocity

The first thing we need to do to solve this problem is to translate it into polar coordinates, and set the angle θ equal to zero at the vertical:

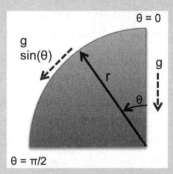

We also need to make some assumption about how fast you are moving to start with (otherwise you will never fall over). In order to keep the

(continued)

comparisons fair, let's say you start off at 2 mph (the speed of a slow walk). If I had been born just a few years earlier, I might have recommended solving this problem by hand using integrals and boundary conditions, but in the spirit of taking every unfair advantage, let's just calculate each little step for each little ramp by throwing it into a spreadsheet:

	A	B	C	D	E	F	G	H	I	J	K
1	Gravitational acceleration (ft./s/s)	32.174									
2	Initial velocity (mph)	2									
3	Radius (ft.)	3									
4											IMPACT!
5	Time (seconds)	0	0.1	0.2	0.3	0.4	0.5	0.6	0.7	0.8	0.9
6	Angle (radians)	0	0.10	0.20	0.31	0.44	0.60	0.78	1.00	1.27	1.59
7	Angular velocity (1/seconds)	0.98	0.98	1.03	1.14	1.30	1.53	1.84	2.21	2.67	3.18
8	Linear velocity (mph)	2.00	2.00	2.11	2.33	2.67	3.14	3.75	4.53	5.45	6.50

When you do the calculations, it turns out the impact velocity for the "planted foot" path is about 6.5 mph, which is significantly slower than the 9.5 mph "free fall" impact velocity. This means if you are throwing or sweeping someone, you can increase the velocity of impact by nearly 50 percent if you take two legs instead of one. It also means if you are the person being thrown, you can reduce the speed at which you hit the floor by 30 percent if you can manage to keep at least one foot on the floor. Of course, there are a large number of tactical differences between the paths as well, such as the increased opportunity to break your fall on the "planted foot" path, but we will not discuss them here.

You can break down a glancing blow by its angle.

If we can use a ramp or a planted foot to break down the force of gravity into a smaller component parallel to the ramp, we should be able to do the same thing for all kinds of forces, including the forces humans generate with their muscles. It turns out a large number of defensive tactics in martial arts employ this principle, where you meet an incoming strike at a diagonal before it has the chance to hit the target head-on. For this example, we will look at two variations on an angled high block, which appear in many

Figure 3-6. Angled roof blocks with a *dao* sword and an eskrima stick. There are many variations on these techniques with different hand placements, and different orientations relative to the body, but the important part is the angled path for your opponent's weapon to follow.

weapons styles, such as wushu, *kendo*, eskrima, and many more. The same principles apply to blocks with any blades, sticks, punches, kicks, or projectiles.

As an incoming strike comes down from overhead, it meets the block at an angle. At this point some of the force of the strike pushes directly into the block, but a significant portion of the force from the strike pushes the striking weapon along the angled surface of the block and away from the intended target. The fraction of the force pushing into the block and the fraction of the force pushing along the block depends on the angle involved, just as the fraction of gravity we feel depends on the steepness of the ramp. This means if you can block at a very steep angle, you will make your opponent spend most of the force of the incoming strike diverting his own weapon, and very little of the force will push into you through the block. Theoretically, this would mean you could have the most efficient blocks by pointing your sword almost directly at your opponent, but the downside of that approach is that your block would not cover very much surface area at such a steep angle. Typically, 45 degrees is a good compromise between efficiency and surface area, but it is good to know anytime you are blocking, if you have an opportunity to steepen your blocking angle without missing the block, you should do it.

Our discussion has focused on forces so far, but momentum can be broken down into components by angles as well. Force and momentum both have a specific direction, and even though forces can come from many different sources (gravity, electric charges repelling each other, your muscles contracting, and many more), they all have the ability to change or generate momentum. Newton's famous second law is often written as $F = ma$ (force equals mass times acceleration), but to be a little more accurate, we should say $F = \partial p / \partial t$, or force equals a change in momentum divided by change in time. This version is not only more accurate for those cases where the mass is allowed to change over time, like a snowplow pushing more and more snow as it moves along, but it also makes sure as you picture forces, your mental image includes momentum, instead of just focusing on acceleration.

Energy does not have a direction, so it cannot be broken down into components like force or momentum. This is why you can reduce the momentum you receive from a blow by taking it at a diagonal, but a bullet will fly through you regardless of the angle of impact.

Advanced concepts: Angles exist in three dimensions.

In order to keep things simple, I restricted all of the examples in this chapter to two dimensions, but in real life, we live in a universe with three spatial dimensions (up/down, left/right, and forward/back). In many cases, two dimensions are sufficient for a simplistic description, because the activity occurs on a single plane, and the orientation of that plane does not change the discussion. In our planted-foot example, your impact velocity is the same whether you fall back or to the side. If we start to look at the details, however, we will see fundamental differences in direction, like how blocking a punch 45 degrees up is different from blocking it 45 degrees to the side because of the direction of gravity and the muscle groups involved. It can be daunting to try to keep three spatial dimensions in mind as you visualize a block, and even more daunting when you include the orientation and handedness of each limb involved, but the human brain is a lot better at spatial understanding than we tend to give it credit for. With a little practice blocking and redirecting your opponent's hands, you can build an intuition for what angle (in all three dimensions) to hold your forearm so his right cross not only moves off to the side, but also rises just enough to leave you an opening under his arm.

CHAPTER 4

Levers, Wedges, and Free Lunches

There are no free lunches.

All of the matter and energy around us can be neither created nor destroyed under normal circumstances, but it can change form. Matter changes into energy under immense gravitational pressure in the giant fusion reactor that is our sun. That solar energy is converted to chemical energy in the leaves of a plant and stored as sugar, the chemical energy from sugar is turned into mechanical energy in your muscles, and that mechanical energy is used to punch people's faces. While it may be awesome that every punch you throw harnesses the power of the sun, the whole process also puts some very real limits on what we are capable of.

When it comes to energy, there really are no free lunches. No matter how hard you try, it is impossible to create or destroy energy. The universe is not a mint that can print free money. It is more like a currency exchange. You can change your dollars into

Figure 4-1. Lunch. This is not free.

euros, euros into yen, and yen back into dollars, but no matter how you change it, you never have more money than you started with. You can change one kind of energy into another kind of energy all day long, but making new energy out of nothing is not possible in our universe.

Levers give up distance for more force.

A lever is a rigid arm that can rotate around a fixed point called a fulcrum, and it allows you to apply a force at one location on the lever and use that force to move an object at a different location on the lever.

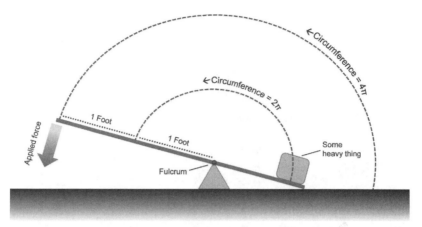

Figure 4-2. Diagram of a simple lever. If you apply a force two feet from the fulcrum, and some heavy thing sits one foot from the fulcrum, the heavy thing moves half your distance, but with twice the force.

Assuming you apply a constant force, you can calculate the energy spent pushing on the lever with the equation $E = F \cdot x$ (energy equals force times distance). Even though we tend to only move a small distance when we use levers, you can see in figure 4-2 that we are actually applying our force along the circumference of a circle. In chapter 3 we learned the circumference of a circle is π times the diameter, so if we apply a force, F, to a lever 2 feet away from the fulcrum (4-foot diameter), and we apply that force over $1/12$ of the circumference of the circle (30 degrees), our total energy spent is

$$E = F_{applied} \frac{4\pi}{12}$$

Since the lever does not bend, we know if we moved $1/12$ of a circle when we applied our force, every point on the lever must have also moved $1/12$ of a circle, including the part of the lever supporting the heavy thing. If we want to calculate the energy spent moving the heavy thing, which is located one foot from the fulcrum (2 feet in diameter) we can write it as

$$E = F_{heavy\ thing}\ \frac{2\pi}{12}$$

Since we cannot create or destroy energy (no free lunches!), then the energy spent pushing on the lever must be equal to the energy spent lifting the heavy thing.

$$F_{applied}\ \frac{4\pi}{12} = F_{heavy\ thing}\ \frac{2\pi}{12}$$

Solving that equation for the force pushing up on the heavy thing gives us

$$F_{heavy\ thing} = 2F_{applied}$$

So when we push on a lever at a distance twice as far from the fulcrum, we can apply twice the force. If we push on a lever at three times the distance from the fulcrum, we can apply three times the force. We can use the this force-distance tradeoff to lift heavy things, like using a car jack to lift a car, or to break sturdy things, like using a crowbar to tear open a padlock or using a bottle opener to open a beer.

The first lesson to learn here is anytime you are applying leverage to your opponent, whether you are controlling his head in a muay Thai clinch or submitting him with *juji gatame* (the classic grappling arm bar), you should do your best to put as much distance as possible between your applied force and the fulcrum. A second, slightly less obvious lesson we can learn is the natural path of any lever is circular, rather than linear, where the distance from the fulcrum determines the size of the circle. The circular path of leverage is incredibly important for small-joint manipulation. If you grab two of your opponent's fingers and pull them back, you may annoy him or cause him to move his arm, but if you twist those same two fingers around in a tight circular path with a fulcrum at the base of the fingers, the pain can drop him to his knees (assuming your opponent is capable of feeling prohibitive pain in this scenario). Another good example where the circular path of a lever is important comes when you catch a kick. If you can grab your opponent's foot during a stand-up fight, you have a lever the size of a human leg at your disposal. For stiff opponents this means you can toss him on his ass with very little effort, just by raising your arm. For flexible opponents with good balance, lifting the kick straight into the air may not cause them any distress, but if you follow the circular path of the lever you have in your hand (up and over toward your opponent), even the most flexible and well-balanced fighters will hit the floor.

You can also turn the lever around and give up force for more distance.

Pushing on the long end of a lever, as in figure 4-2, is a great way to increase the force you apply to your opponent, but increasing force is only one of many paths you can take in a fight. A force is what allows us to give something (or someone) momentum, so we can think of a force like a push. A push can be helpful in a fight, but if you care more about impact velocity than the "push" of your attack, you can flip your lever around and use it in the opposite direction.

If you apply your force at a distance of one foot from the fulcrum, as in figure 4-3, you will not have enough force to lift heavy things, but you can definitely smack your opponent in the face with the long end of the lever (two feet from the fulcrum). If we use the same calculations from the previous section (energy equals force times distance, and energy is the same on both ends of the lever), we find the force at the long end of the lever is only half the force you applied at the short end, but the distance traveled at the long end of the lever is twice the distance traveled at the short end. By itself, double the distance is not incredibly useful, but if you keep in mind that both ends of the lever move at the same

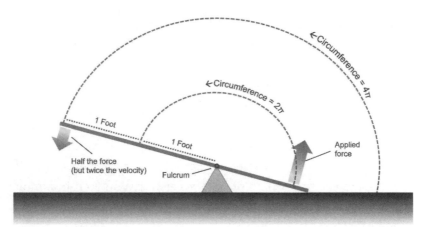

Figure 4-3. The same lever from figure 4-2, but now there is no heavy object to lift, and the force you apply is close to the fulcrum (one foot away). The far end of the lever (two feet away) will only move with half of the applied force, but it must travel twice the distance in the same amount of time, so it has twice the velocity.

time, this means the long end of the lever must travel at twice the speed in order to cover that distance in the same amount of time.

A good example of this type of lever at work is the old slapstick comedy "step on a rake" gag. The gag unfolds as an unsuspecting person steps on the short end of a rigid rake (the applied force is his weight), and the much longer end of the rake rotates up and smacks the person in the face—or the balls, depending on the length of the rake. There is not nearly enough force to push the victim back, but it is still difficult to watch without cringing in sympathy.

The muscles that move our limbs all use levers to trade force for speed in this same way. The muscles connect very close to the fulcrum (your joint), but the movement they generate happens at the far end of the bone they are pulling. This means you can move your hands and feet much faster than your muscles themselves are capable of contracting on their own. This also means your muscles can apply much more force closer to the joints than far away. To test this out, next time you bring the groceries into the house,

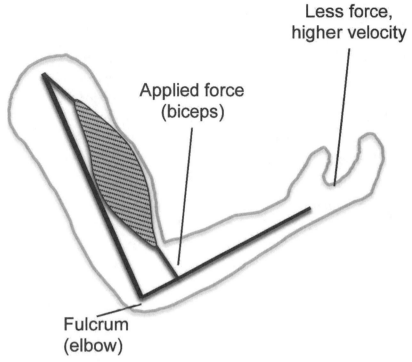

Figure 4-4. Diagram of the biceps as a lever. The force is applied much closer to the fulcrum than the hands, so our hands are able move faster than our muscles can contract, but with significantly less force.

carry one bag in each hand, with your elbows locked at a 90-degree angle. Next slide your hands through the handles and let the bags hang halfway up your forearms. This should feel much easier on your biceps.

Many weapons in martial arts make this same exchange. Since your arms are already levers with your muscles at the short end and your opponent at the long end, when you place an eskrima stick or a long sword in your hand, you are just farther extending the length of that lever. Considering many sticks and swords are similar in length to an extended human arm (about 30 inches), we can generalize and say strikes with these weapons can travel at roughly twice the velocity as a similar empty-handed strike.

Wedges exchange one direction for another.

While a lever lets you make trade-offs between force and distance, a wedge lets you take a force in one direction, divide it in two, and send it off in two different directions. Lumberjacks use wedges all the time to split wood, because not only is it easier for the human body to apply force perpendicular to the surface of the wood, but if the wedge is narrow enough (a very small angle at the point), it can also increase the force applied—in exchange for some distance, of course.

Wing chun involves the concept of "wedging out" punches more often than other styles because it uses a square-shouldered stance instead of keeping the power hand back. This means any incoming strikes that happen to travel along the outside of the arms will be redirected away from the head without the need for active blocking. In muay Thai clinch fighting, you use the same wedging process to get your arms on the inside and gain control of your opponent. The "cross counter" is another example of wedging that has been used successfully in boxing and MMA. There are many variations to the technique, but the basic premise involves extending your right cross over the top of your opponent's left jab. Since your shoulder is below your head, a successful cross counter will direct the jab down and away from your head as your fist approaches your opponent's chin. If you want a simple example to test out using a wedge at home, have a friend of similar height

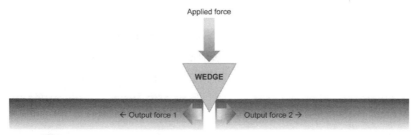

Figure 4-5. Diagram of a wedge. The applied force comes in from above and is split in two separate output forces, each pushing away from the wedge.

approach you with two arms outstretched, as if to do the Hollywood-style two-hands-on-the-windpipe choke. As he approaches you, keep your shoulders square and extend your own arms, reaching for his neck or face, while ensuring your hands are on the inside. As he gets closer, the shape of your extended arms will clear his hands away from your neck, and you will be free to put your hands in his face.

If you steal someone else's lunch it is "free" to you.

Even though the universe does not allow you to create energy from nothing, there are no restrictions on where the energy comes from. For most punches and kicks we throw, the energy comes from our own calories digested and absorbed from food (calories are just a unit of energy), but if you are presented with the right scenarios, there are a number of situations where you can spend your opponent's calories instead of your own. Technically, it is not free energy, but it is "free" to you.

If you were to push a boulder up a hill, it might take a long time, and you would probably burn a ton of calories, but once you got to the top of the hill, you could let the boulder go and watch all those calories turn into kinetic energy as it tumbles down the hill. When we spend energy to put an object into a precarious position, either with regard to gravity or some other force, we say we have given it potential energy, which is just a shorthand way of saying we spent energy arranging the scenario, and we expect to redeem that energy at some later point in time. We give ourselves potential energy every time we stand up, and we redeem that energy later on as we sit or lie down. If you want to get a feel for how much energy goes into standing up, lie down on your back and pay close attention to your muscles as you rise to your feet. Chances are you use your abdominal muscles to sit up while pushing on the floor with one hand, and then rise from the floor by pushing with one hand and two feet. This is much more energy than you can pack into a single punch, and if you ever trip or have your feet swept out from under you, this is exactly how much energy you will redeem as you fall to the floor. The "free to you" part of all this is if you knock your opponent over, you are using his potential energy and not your own. If he is going to get back up, he will have to use his own calories to do so. The advantages of using your opponent's energy become even more pronounced when facing a larger opponent because the energy it takes for him to stand up increases with every pound of weight and every inch of height.

Another more immediate way to spend your opponent's energy instead of your own is to respond to your opponent's incoming linear push with rotational motion. The best way to picture this is if your opponent is in a revolving door and he pushes the door in front of him hard enough, he will get smacked in the ass with the door as it rotates around the center. Punches can be too quick or too nonlinear to take advantage of in this manner, but a slow, one-handed push to the shoulder is the perfect opportunity to spend your opponent's energy, and it is easy enough for a novice fighter to try. Have a friend push you with one hand on your shoulder, just hard enough to make you take a step or two back. Stay stiff and keep both shoulders square to him as he does. After a few pushes, allow yourself to rotate around your center like a revolving door. You can even rotate yourself on purpose if you want to spend a little bit of your own energy too. You should find it relatively easy to stand your ground now, and you will no longer need to take a step back. After a few more pushes, extend the arm attached to the opposite shoulder and push your friend back. With a few more pushes it should be obvious to both you and your friend who is spending the majority of the calories (your friend) and who is feeling most of the push (also your friend).

Another great way to spend your opponent's calories is to use the "tug-of-war" trick, which is a trick many of us learned the hard

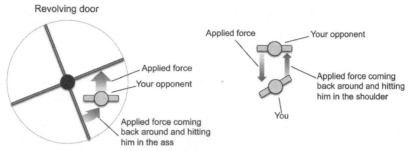

Figure 4-6. Rotational redirection of your opponent's force. **Left:** Diagram of a revolving door as seen from above. As your opponent pushes the door, he spends his energy rotating the structure about the center, which then causes the door behind him to hit him in the ass. **Right:** Diagram of the redirection of a single-arm push as seen from above. Your opponent pushes on your shoulder, which rotates you around your center and results in a push back into your opponent with the opposite hand.

way as children. In order to play tug-of-war, you and a friend agree to pull a rope in opposite directions. Whoever can pull the rope hard enough to make the other person cross the starting line is the winner. The trick comes when you decide you don't care who wins, and you would rather just watch your friend topple over, so you let go of the rope. Your friend, who was spending as much energy as he could trying to pull you, no longer feels any resistance and falls to the ground.

This trick comes up across many different martial arts styles. In both judo and wrestling, the tug-of-war trick is a great pre-amble to a sacrifice throw, where your opponent leans into you, but instead of pushing back, you just take a seat on the floor (and possibly stick your foot into his stomach, depending on the throw). In some striking styles such as kenpo or muay Thai, if your opponent blocks your punch to the inside with too much force, you can let your arm go limp at the elbow. This can lead to your opponent clearing his own opening for that elbow of yours, which is already halfway there by now. This same block sensitivity is an important part of *chi sao* drills in wing chun and jeet kune do. These drills work by maintaining hand contact and feeling for excessive pressure in any direction from your opponent, before ultimately allowing your opponent to move his own hand out of the way with that excessive pressure while you strike.

Stealing a free lunch is wonderful, and there is some ironic "stop hitting yourself" justice to it, but just like any other kind of theft, stealing a free lunch during a fight is a crime of opportunity, and there is no guarantee you will have that chance. You should approach any situation prepared to spend your own energy to get out of it, but if your opponent is going to leave his lunch sitting on the table, you should definitely eat it. Personally, when I fight or train, I like to make a mental note anytime I feel my opponent and I are pushing against each other. It doesn't always mean it's time for the tug-of-war trick, but chances are, if you are in a force-on-force scenario, there is probably something more productive you could be doing instead of just pushing back.

Advanced concepts: A fulcrum is rarely stationary in a fight.

For the sake of explaining the physics involved, we can use figure 4-2 as our example, but in a scenario where your opponent would rather not be on the receiving end of your leverage, it can get complicated. In the case of a standing arm bar there is no stationary point to use as a fulcrum, so you need to apply two separate forces to make it work (pull up on the wrist, and push down just above the elbow). When it comes to the juji gatame, there are at least three distinct applied forces at play: pulling back on the arm at the wrist, pushing your opponent's shoulders down on the mat by extending your legs, and extending your hips upward to raise the fulcrum at the same time. In order to keep all this straight in our heads with so much going on, we need to break it down into pieces. Every point of contact you have with your opponent has a purpose. When you are training a technique that uses leverage in one form or another, go through each point of contact with your opponent and ask yourself if this is meant to be a firm (possibly moving) fulcrum, an applied force, or a preventive measure against an escape or counterattack. Even the most complicated techniques boil down to basic components.

Advanced concepts: Currency exchanges always charge a small fee.

Just like currency exchanges charge a small fee for their services, anytime you change energy from one form to another in real life, you almost always end up with just a little bit less than what you put in. The levers in figure 4-2 and figure 4-3 are not weightless, so you have to have enough energy to move the lever by itself before you can even think about what happens on the other end of the lever. Friction occurs at the fulcrum, so you need to spend more energy there. If you are using a lever to increase your velocity, you need to spend more energy pushing the air out of the way as you move. As a general rule, air resistance is a significant factor anytime you can hear your strike moving through the air. For most of our purposes, you can ignore these small fees, but it always helps to understand the points at which our assumptions begin to break down.

Advanced concepts: Levers that bend are called springs.

Another way some of our assumptions can break down has to do with the rigidity of our lever. If the lever breaks, then you end up spending your energy causing structural damage to the lever instead of lifting heavy things. If the lever bends but does not break, we have an interesting scenario where the lever acts as a spring and temporarily stores a portion of the energy you spend. In either case you will end up spending energy on the lever itself, and not on your opponent.

SECTION 2
Protect Yourself with Knowledge

CHAPTER 5

Knockouts and Brain Damage in Athletes

Brain damage is an invisible killer.

Professional fighters, American football players, hockey players, and even members of the military are all at high risk for a relatively enigmatic disorder called chronic traumatic encephalopathy, or CTE. CTE is a neurodegenerative disorder (meaning your brain slowly degrades over time) caused by repeated blows to the head. Dr. Harrison Stanford Martland first identified it as "punch drunk" syndrome in 1928, when he noticed many retired professional boxers displayed similar behavioral symptoms (Martland, 1928). "Punch drunk" eventually became the more formal sounding *dementia pugilistica* (Millspaugh, 1937), but very little was known about the disorder. The name "CTE" had been around since sometime in the 1960s, but it did not really catch on until some fairly recent autopsies performed on American football players revealed that athletes in all collision sports are at high risk for the same neurodegenerative disorder originally identified in boxers (Omalu,

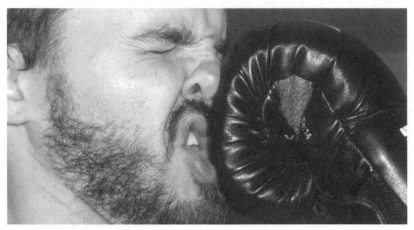

Figure 5-1. Brain damage in action.

DeKosky, Minster, Kamboh, Hamilton, & Wecht, 2005; McKee, et al., 2009).

Even today CTE is still not very well understood. The only way to diagnose CTE is through autopsy because the damage is not visible on traditional CT scans or MRIs, and the symptoms vary from individual to individual. The injury occurs at a subconcussive level, meaning you could develop CTE even if you have never been knocked out or received a concussion. In addition, most athletes and fighters do not even start to develop symptoms until five or ten years after retirement. Fortunately, scientists have been making significant progress toward the ability to diagnose CTE in living patients. New MRI techniques, called "diffusion tensor imaging" (Mayer, et al., 2010), may help us better identify changes in the brain after injury, and new PET scan techniques using special molecular markers (Small, et al., 2013) may be able to detect the buildup of tau proteins in the brain, a telltale sign of CTE. Diagnosing CTE in living athletes will open doors, allowing us to perform analysis over the course of a career, across sports, and more, but for now, we will have to deal with the fact that this disorder is very difficult to identify while the athlete is still alive.

Brain damage hurts more than just your IQ.

Twice a year the Dog Brothers host a full-contact stick-fighting event in Los Angeles called a Gathering of the Pack. The event brings in fighters from around the country looking to test their skills in a realistic setting, and participation is considered a rite of passage for many stick fighters. Every gathering begins with some "magic words" from Marc "Crafty Dog" Denny:

> *No judges, no referees, no trophies. One rule only: Be friends at the end of the day. This means our goal is that no one spends the night in the hospital. Our goal is that everyone leaves with the IQ with which they came. No suing no one for no reason for nothing no how no way! Real contact stick fighting is dangerous and only you are responsible for you, so protect yourself at all times.*

Of course, the statement about leaving with the same IQ you showed up with is meant to help fighters maintain the appropriate level of respect for each other's safety during the fights, but it also captures a mental picture of brain damage that is familiar to fighters of all martial arts styles, and even from athletes in other contact sports.

Since our brain is where we do our thinking, we tend to assume damage to the brain means we will get a slightly lower score on that next math test for each punch we take to the face. The English language also plays a big role in reinforcing this point of view. If someone calls you "brainy" or says you have a "big brain," it is understood that person is implying you are smart, but in fact, the brain does much more than math problems. The brain is where you interpret the world, communicate with others, control the muscles of your body, and even feel emotions. Most everything we attribute to your "personality" or your "heart" actually occurs in the brain. In fact, if you want to bring a little science into your relationship, next Valentine's Day, when you give or receive a heart-shaped gift, politely remind your significant other that the heart just pumps blood. Your brain is where the "love" is.

While the symptoms of CTE can include difficulty with math or memory, some common early symptoms also include disorientation, dizziness, headaches, irritability, outbursts of violent or aggressive behavior, confusion, speech abnormalities, and major depressive disorder (McKee, et al., 2009). A large number of CTE symptoms have very little to do with how "smart" you are, and CTE can make daily life or maintaining simple human relationships extremely difficult. A disproportionately large number of retired athletes with CTE commit suicide, including Chicago Bears defensive back Dave Duerson, who texted his family to ask that his brain be used for research into the disease before fatally shooting himself in the chest in 2011.

CTE starts with rotational motion.

In the 1950s and 1960s scientists carried out experiments on corpses and animals to determine the extent to which a human could withstand an incoming blow to the forehead from a flat surface of a hard material (Gurdjian, Roberts, & Thomas, 1966; Eiband, 1959). This experimentation looked at linear acceleration of the head as a function of time, focusing on easily identifiable injuries such as skull fractures, and led to the development of the Gadd Severity Index (GSI) and the Head Injury Criterion (HIC), which we still use to evaluate helmets today (Gadd, 1966; Versace, 1971). The (outdated) assumption behind the safety gear we use in boxing, martial arts, American football, and many other contact sports is that a concussion (or the subconcussive damage that leads to CTE) is just the result of a less extreme version of the linear accelerations that lead to skull fractures.

Over time it has become clear that the linear view of head injury is not appropriate for understanding concussions or CTE. Boxing gloves and football helmets are both relatively successful at reducing the sudden linear acceleration of the skull on impact, but neither appears able to measurably reduce the occurrence of CTE in athletes. Much of the modern research done now reflects a rotational model for brain injury (Smith & Meaney, Axonal damage in traumatic brain injury, 2000), and since the mid 2000s, the scientific and medical communities have (more or less) come to a consensus view that the primary mechanism behind the type of brain injury that leads to CTE is a sudden rotational accelera-tion of the head (King, Yang, Zhang, Hardy, & Viano, 2003). Of course, all of this scientific progress only told us what boxers had already known for years: if you are trying to knock someone out, a left hook to the chin is far more effective than a straight punch to the forehead.

The microscopic culprit: Diffuse axonal injury

The details on how these injuries occur at the cellular level are dif-ficult to study, mostly due to the fact that we cannot positively identify the damage on conventional scans, but since the adoption of the rotational view of brain injury, a process called "diffuse axo-nal injury" has emerged as the most likely mechanism behind CTE (Johnson, Stewart, & Smith, 2013). Diffuse axonal injury occurs when some of the axons (long nerve fibers) in your brain feel a rapid stretching force beyond the scope of typical voluntary movement, and as a result, the axons become damaged. Scientists are still investigating the nature of the damage itself, but the long-term result appears to be a slow buildup of transport materials over time into an "axonal bulb," which ultimately ends with a com-plete disconnection of the axon. It is only after there have been a significant number of disconnected axons, years after the initial injuries, that the symptoms of CTE become apparent.

Even severe cases of traumatic brain injury damage only a small percentage of axons (Johnson, Stewart, & Smith, 2013), but once an axon has been damaged, it can no longer provide the same physical resistance to an applied force, implying the more diffuse axonal injury an athlete suffers, the easier it becomes to suffer similar injuries in the future. Age is often a confounding factor you need to account for as well, but Chuck Liddell is a prime example of how this can happen in real life. Throughout his twenty-three-fight career spanning twelve years, he took punches from some of the greatest fighters in MMA history, but he finally retired in 2010 after three consecutive losses by knockout from blows he could have (possibly) shaken off earlier in his career.

There is still much more we need to learn about diffuse axonal injury and CTE, but the medical community has been giving a promising amount of attention to the issue in recent years. In the near future we may be able to detect the extent of the damage sustained in a fight or during practice, and we may even be able to treat or reverse the damage before it results in full disconnection of an axon. Alternatively, we may be able to take preventive measures to protect our axons, either chemically or through a new generation of safety gear specifically designed to reduce diffuse axonal injury.

The physics of diffuse axonal injury

Given our understanding of the rotational nature of diffuse axonal injury, it is now possible for us to take what we learned about levers and rotational motion in the previous chapters and apply that knowledge here to help us understand how a punch to the chin ends up stretching and damaging axons in the brainstem and throughout the brain.

The first step in this process is the punch. This punch must meet a minimum energy requirement because we will be causing structural damage to axons in the brain. This punch must also meet a minimum momentum requirement because we need to spin the whole head around to damage those axons. Considering what we

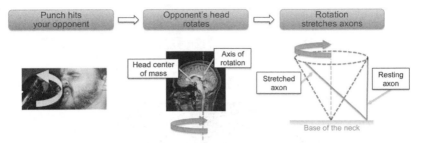

Figure 5-2. The process of diffuse axonal injury from punch to axon stretching. **Left:** The punch hits your opponent. **Center:** The punch rotates your opponent's head around an axis located in the neck. **Right:** Axons located a small distance from the axis of rotation become stretched as one end of the axon travels around the axis of rotation.

know about knockout punches and how boxers train, it is relatively safe to say that meeting the minimum energy requirement is not difficult, but meeting the minimum momentum requirement is. Fast punches are important strategically, but increasing the effective mass behind your punches is what gives your punch the ability to lay your opponent out on the mat.

This story takes us from the fist to the axon, but there is still something missing. We turn our heads left and right every day, sometimes very rapidly, so what makes a punch so special? The science is still too young to be sure, but I will speculate that the peak of the force curve (figure 5-3) is typically where the axon gets rapidly extended to its natural limit, but the tail of the force curve is where the axons are damaged.

The primary reason for this speculation is the empirical knowledge that pushing off the back foot is essential for a good knockout punch. Boxers and martial artists from all styles stress the importance of this push to the success of a punch. Some strikes, such as a front-hand palm strike or a square-shouldered wing chun punch, for which a back-foot push is impossible, will still generate the same long-tail force profile in figure 5-3 by making contact before the arm is fully extended and using the muscles in the arm

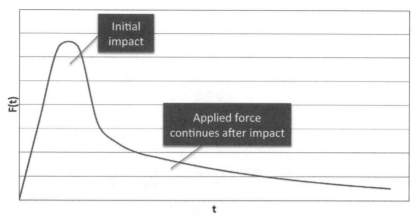

Figure 5-3. The force of a punch over time. The initial impact is where we see the "peak force," but the longer tail comes from the follow-through and the push off the back foot. The peak may only last for a few milliseconds, but the tail can continue for longer than a second, depending on the situation at hand.

to apply force by continuing the extension. The same profile appears when athletes tackle each other in other contact sports. There is an initial peak force at the moment of collision, but the legs continue to push after the initial peak.

Another reason the tail is a good candidate for the damage done is because it is a region of relatively constant force you generate with your muscles, and you even use a lever when you apply the force to the axons in your opponent's brain. That lever is your opponent's face.

As you may remember from our discussion of levers in chapter 4, objects sitting close to the center of rotation will feel the most force, and objects sitting twice as far away will feel half the force. Of course, the calculation of force here is a bit more complicated than a simple lever because different parts of your brain will feel different amounts of leverage, but the same basic principles still apply. It could be these internal differences in forces, along with different densities and shapes inside the brain that lead to the specific type of axonal damage we see in CTE.

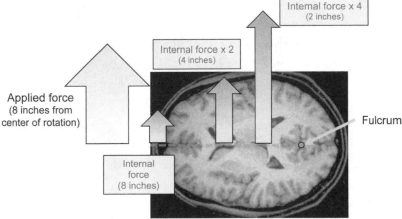

Figure 5-4. A top view of a brain with an applied force to the chin. The head rotates around the neck at the base of the skull. The force felt at points close to the center of rotation will be much higher than the force felt farther away. This is, of course, a very simplified view.

Just because the back-foot push is important doesn't necessarily mean it is essential for diffuse axonal injury. We may find out the axons are damaged instantaneously, and that push is just for controlling and disorienting your opponent. We will have to wait for the science to mature and tell us how the details of the process work, but until we know for sure, I am going to practice my right cross with a strong push from my back foot.

The neck is also a viable target.

Given our understanding of diffuse axonal injury as the result of stretching forces on the axons in the brain (particularly near the base of the skull), it is reasonable to assume you could generate the same damage by applying a force on either side of the same axon. Since it appears that knockouts occur as a result of diffuse axonal injury involving the brainstem (Smith, et al., 2000), we should be able to apply our force to the neck to get a knockout as well. Of course, if you land a left hook to the chin, you get to use the head as a lever, but there are no levers for the neck, so you will have to apply more force to your strike in order to get the same result. We can see this in action in muay Thai, MMA, and kickboxing matches, where a kick to the side of the neck can cause an opponent to lose consciousness immediately. Strikes directly to the back of the head (at the base of the skull) generate the same effect, but the minimum force required is lower, possibly because there is less muscle and other tissue between the axons and the point of impact. These strikes are illegal in most styles of fighting for sport, but they are still good to know, just in case you find yourself in a life-or-death scenario with an opportunity to strike there.

Use your brain to knock out your opponent.

Now that we have a basic understanding of diffuse axonal injury, the obvious next question is, "How can I use this knowledge to become a better fighter?" Sometimes the right visualization of the process is all it takes so give your training a significant edge. When you throw a punch, think about how your punch will rotate your opponent's head. If you give your opponent a linear palm strike to the face, you will probably do a lot of damage to your opponent, but if you can strike and then move your hand up and over, forcing your opponent to look up at the ceiling, you will probably have a better chance of knockout from that strike.

Another way to adjust your training is to practice hitting something that can rotate. Some heavy bags or double-end bags can rotate when you hit them, or you can try out the Quest Training AllStrike, which functions much like a focus mitt in the shape of a human head for fine-tuning your targeting, but it also provides realistic rotational feedback. If you can start understanding when you are spinning a head versus when you are pushing it back, you are on your way to being a better knockout artist.

It is also good to remember high-energy strikes, like snap punches or strikes with weapons like an eskrima stick, are definitely not knockout blows. They can be incredibly damaging and they can end a fight immediately, but they will not generate diffuse axonal injury, unless they also happen to carry enough momentum to move a human head. A baseball bat, however, or a club you can put your weight behind is still capable of knocking someone out.

The other side of this same pursuit of knowledge is the question, "How can I avoid hurting the people I train with?" Many muay Thai schools will practice elbow and knee strikes with pads, but they will not use elbows or knees in sparring. Those techniques are saved for pads or the ring only. I propose we do the same thing with strikes designed specifically to rotate the head. Try your best to rotate the head when you practice on pads, but when you are sparring with your training partners, try to keep the head motion you induce with your punches relatively linear. Will this intentional flaw in your training cause you to miss an opportunity to knock out an opponent in the ring? Possibly. Is it worth giving your training partners permanent brain damage to make sure you train like you fight? Definitely not.

CTE ruins lives.

Discussing the permanent loss of mental functions, depression, and many other symptoms of a degenerative disease with no known treatment or cure is a sobering topic, particularly for aspiring professional fighters who have to consider the possibility that by the time they are in their forties, their quality of life may be so poor, the world will pity them despite their successes. The American Medical Association, like many other national medical associations around the globe, has called for a ban on boxing as a sport, and every few years it renews this request, just to be clear its stance is still firm.

We all understand there is a certain risk of injury or death for athletes in any sport. Part of the respect we have for athletes comes from the knowledge that they face these dangers willingly. It takes incredible willpower to get out on the field knowing there is always a chance you might need to be carried off, and it takes a tremendous amount of strength just to step into the ring with a trained fighter who is convinced that punching your face is his ticket to success. Despite this understanding, there is still something inherently unfair about CTE. For other types of injuries, like broken bones or torn ligaments, the pain is immediate, and the athlete knows he has made a mistake. He learns from his mistakes, and he will probably take some time off to recover so he can compete again. For CTE there is very little pain (thanks to the safety gear we wear), the damage accumulates undetected over the course of a career, and there is no lesson to be learned. CTE is the thanks our athletes get for a long career of playing hard.

My grandmaster in hapkido had a black-belt student at his school who had been studying under him for nearly thirty years. He told us this student was a handsome and bright young man when they first met, and he was one of the best fighters he had ever trained. This student got into a lot of fights on the streets, spent a lot of time behind bars as a result, and then got into even more fights when he was locked up. It is always tough to tell how true some stories are, but supposedly, this student had taken on as many as twelve guys at a time and walked away from it. When I first met him, he was in his late forties, missing most of his teeth, had one bad eye, and was unable to follow a simple conversation, even if it directly involved him. He couldn't remember any of the advanced techniques, and he would get angry and yell regularly. Sometimes in sparring (especially if he took a punch to the face), he would forget where he was and start going full force like his life depended on it. This student was suffering from more than just CTE, and I often wondered why my grandmaster kept him around. Was he meant to serve as an example to us that too much experience in the ring or on the street would ruin our lives? Was it because he still saw the shadow of that young man he taught thirty years earlier and could not bear to turn him away? I will never know for sure, but I'd like to think it was a little bit of each.

CHAPTER 6

Foam or Knuckles— Navigating the Illusion of Safety

It is difficult to say when boxing gloves made their first appearance. A relief called *Boxing Boys* from Thera, Greece, provides evidence for gloved boxing as far back as 1600 BCE, but we usually credit Jack Broughton, the bareknuckle champion of England throughout the 1730s, with the introduction of modern Western-style boxing gloves, which he called "mufflers." Mufflers were ten-ounce leather gloves padded with horsehair or lamb's wool, and they were intended to keep the wealthy students who attended his boxing school from getting black eyes or bloody noses. In 1867 John Graham Chambers, a Welsh sportsman and journalist, attempted to clean up the image of boxing, which had become tarnished from decades of gambling, corruption, fixed matches, and riots. With the support of the Marquess of Queensberry, he published a set of formalized rules, which included the mandatory

Figure 6-1. Boxing gloves, MMA gloves, and bare knuckles.

use of gloves. Even then many boxers did not embrace the "Queensbury rules" until 1892, when "Gentleman Jim" Corbett finally knocked out the longtime undefeated world bareknuckle boxing champion, John L. Sullivan, a.k.a. "The Boston Strong Boy," in a gloved match under the Queensbury rules. While protection from black eyes and bloody noses played an important role in the adoption of boxing gloves, this sensational knockout of a legendary fighter legitimized gloved boxing for participants and spectators alike.

Sometime around 1929 King Rama VII of Thailand, who had attended Eton College and Woolwich Military Academy in England before serving six years in the British army, drew inspiration from the Queensbury rules of boxing, and developed a new set of rules and weight classes for muay Thai. These new rules included the use of Western-style gloves, and they transformed the sport considerably. The style of fighting prior to these changes, now called *muay boran*, varied regionally within the country and featured a low, wide stance and a broad range of techniques. Fighters dropped many old techniques as they adopted the new rules, and the stance (and hands) of the fighters shifted higher to the modern stance we see today. It is interesting to note that the stance (and hands) of Western boxing underwent a similar transformation as its practitioners adopted the Queensbury rules and donned boxing gloves. Even today most Americans can imitate an "old timey" bareknuckle boxing stance if you ask them to.

When UFC 1 debuted in 1993, the competitors fought without gloves, with the exception of the professional boxer Art Jimmerson, who decided to fight with one boxing glove and one free hand (so he could tap out, if necessary). Jimmerson's opponent, Royce Gracie, wasted no time in taking the fight to the mat, where Jimmerson tapped out even before Gracie had a chance to apply a submission. At UFC 4 (1994) another professional boxer, Milton Bowen, became the first MMA fighter to wear two fingerless gloves in the UFC, similar to the ones used today. He lost his fight by submission as well, but ironically, his opponent, Steve Jennum, was unable to continue to the next round because he had hurt his hands during the match and was no longer able to make a fist. UFC 6 (1995) featured David "Tank" Abbott, a 270-pound "pit fighter" who learned to fight by brawling in the streets and in bars. Abbott famously claimed to have been fighting back when the prize for winning was going to jail, and he made fingerless gloves popular over the next few years with a series of powerful knockouts. His fight with the four-hundred-pound John Matua lasted only eighteen seconds. In 1996 Senator John McCain (R-Arizona), a lifelong boxing fan, saw footage of a UFC fight and began a campaign against the "barbaric" sport. He wrote letters to the governors of all fifty states, resulting in a thirty-six-state ban on "no holds barred" fighting, and cable companies began to drop UFC events from their pay-per-view lineups. The UFC nearly collapsed under this pressure, and responded by introducing a number of changes to help portray MMA as a legitimate sport, including weight classes, five-minute rounds, bans on some of the more dangerous techniques, and required use of MMA gloves for all fighters (starting with UFC 14 in 1997). While most states have since reversed their positions, as of this writing the ban is still in place in New York.

It was the desire to appear civilized that led to the adoption of gloves for both boxing and MMA, rather than a genuine need to address fighter safety, and both had spectacular knockouts to make them popular. This may have been the case for muay Thai as well, but we can only speculate on King Rama VII's motivations. Today insurance companies and athletic commissions around the globe have turned this superficial tradition into a legal mandate, citing safety as their concern. If we really want to understand how gloves contribute to the safety of our athletes, especially when it comes to their brains, we should take a closer look at the physics behind taking a punch with a bare fist or a glove.

A large surface area is good for dispersing energy.

The surface area of a boxing glove is obviously much larger than that of a bare fist, but it is difficult to appreciate the magnitude of the difference without first doing some experimentation. I have made some measurements of my own fists in action to help shed some light on these differences, but I encourage you to try it out yourself, using your own fists and your own gloves.

The method I followed was relatively simple in nature, but a little tedious in practice. First I attached a paper towel to a body opponent bag. Any punching bag or "realistic" target will do. Next I applied a coat of red acrylic paint to my hand, using a sponge to apply the paint evenly, and punched the target at full force.

I performed this process ten times with bare knuckles, boxing gloves, and MMA gloves. I measured a bunch of other strikes as well, primarily for the sake of my own curiosity. I also threw some punches at a hardwood floor so we could see the difference between hard and soft targets. After all the punching was done, I took a picture of the imprinted paper towels with a ruler in the shot for reference. I obtained the surface area by counting the number of pixels per inch along the ruler, and then counting the red pixels in each imprint of my fist.

Punching the hardwood floor resulted in an imprint of the first two knuckles (1.7 square inches), which aligns with our own visualization of a punch when we throw it, but the introduction

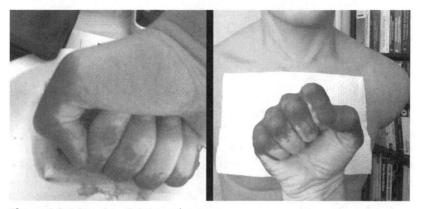

Figure 6-2. Instructions: Paint, punch, repeat.

of a soft target resulted in a full imprint of the fist (8.8 square inches, including some of the thumb). The boxing glove covered a surface area almost three times larger than the fist (23.6 square inches), but the MMA glove was only larger by about 20 percent (10.3 square inches).

These results are interesting, but we should consider them as rough estimates and not hard data. Every fist and every glove is a little different, so I encourage you to test your own at home. Additionally, we should remember humans are a combination of hard and soft targets, so even though MMA gloves have a 20 percent larger surface area when compared to a right cross on a soft target, the surface area of the MMA glove would be six times greater than a right cross to a hard surface.

These measurements are important to us because a larger surface area reduces localized tissue damage. As we learned back in chapter 2, the energy of a strike can be spent on structural damage to the surrounding tissue, and the momentum of a strike determines how much you can move your opponent (or your opponent's head). Surface area has no effect on momentum, but it is incredibly important when it comes to dispersing energy. The sharp side of a knife has a very small surface area, which can cause

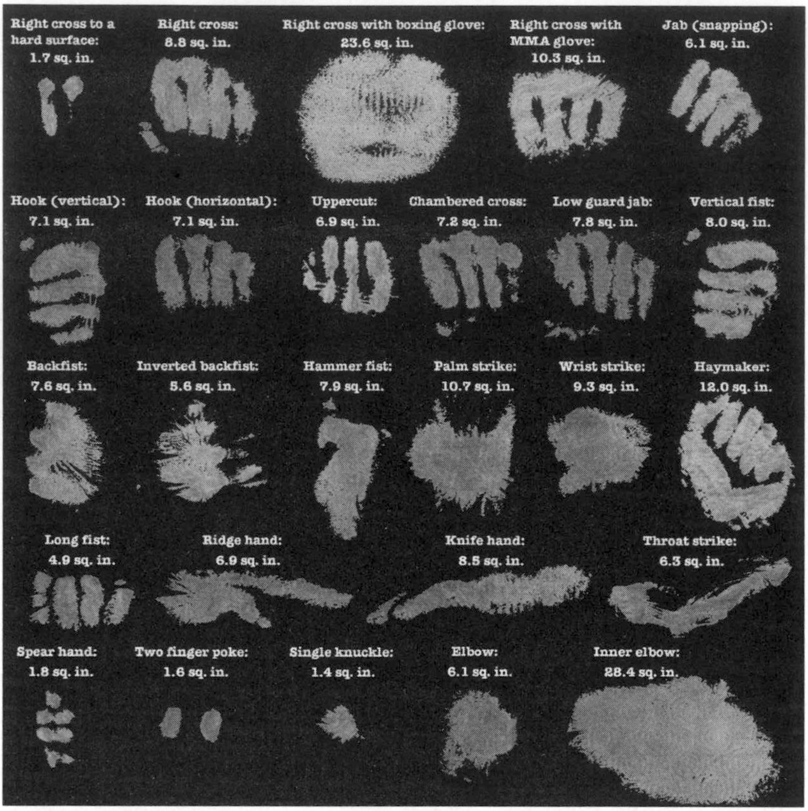

Figure 6-3. The surface area for twenty-six different types of strikes with the hands, as measured using paint transfer on a body opponent bag.

devastating local damage to your tissue, but the flat side of the knife has a large surface area, which is relatively harmless. This implies that gloves with large surface areas should be effective at reducing the type of superficial injuries associated with local tissue damage, so we should expect to see more cuts, bruises, black eyes, and swelling during an MMA match than we would during a boxing match. Anecdotally, this seems to be the case, and a cursory Google Images search for postfight faces would appear to agree, but there are no reliable statistics we can use to make definitive comparisons of the gloves alone, due to a large number of other key differences between the sports.

Conclusion: Gloves with large surface areas disperse energy and reduce the frequency and severity of cuts, bruises, swelling, black eyes, and other localized tissue injuries. Momentum transfer is unaffected, which means a large surface area provides no protection from diffuse axonal injury to the brain.

Foam padding is good for absorbing energy.

The compression of padding in boxing gloves and MMA gloves requires energy. When this energy is spent compressing foam, it is no longer available to compress your opponent's face. Much like the surface area, we would expect this to result in a reduction in localized tissue damage, but the foam will have no effect on the momentum transfer. You can test this personally by pushing a friend or a punching bag with your bare knuckles, and then doing it again with a glove on. The primary noticeable difference in the pushes comes from the slight change in the length of your reach.

Conclusion: Gloves with lots of padding absorb energy as the pads compress, which reduces the frequency and severity of cuts, bruises, swelling, and black eyes. Momentum transfer is unaffected, which means padding provides no protection from diffuse axonal injury to the brain.

Greater plasticity means "glancing" blows are solid.

When you punch your opponent on the chin while wearing boxing gloves (and to a much lesser extent, MMA gloves), the padding in the glove compresses around the chin, and the outer shape of the glove conforms to the shape of your opponent's face. Not only does this increase the surface area, but it also allows for the transfer of momentum from a punch that might have otherwise been deflected. In chapter 3 we learned you can use angles to break up force or momentum into two different components, and some of the most effective blocks employ steep angles so only a small fraction of the momentum of your opponent's incoming punch gets transferred to you. When it comes to boxing gloves, the shape of the glove changes to push your opponent's face instead of just deflecting away, and that makes it easier to transfer your punch momentum to his head.

Conclusion: Gloves with lots of padding will increase surface area for glancing blows, reducing superficial damage, but they may also increase the transfer of momentum. This may be a minor effect, however, as it only applies to glancing blows.

Covered fingers mean fewer eye injuries.

The tips of your fingers have a very small surface area, and when that small surface area meets the soft tissue of the eye, it takes very little energy to do serious damage. Boxing gloves provide a significant advantage here because all of the fingers are contained in the glove. Even though MMA rules forbid eye gouging, accidental eye injury is still very common. Some athletes have complained that the flat shape of the padding in MMA gloves extends the fingers when the hand is at rest, which may make MMA gloves, not bare fists, more likely to cause eye injury. The UFC is looking for a solution to this problem because the audience and both fighters go home unhappy when a fight ends in an accidental eye injury, but for now, this remains an outstanding issue with MMA gloves.

Conclusion: Gloves with covered fingers significantly reduce the rate of eye injury.

Fist compression and stabilization reduce hand injuries.

Both boxing and MMA gloves are worn with hand wraps. While this does provide some padding, the key benefits to wrapping the hand come from stability and compression. When you strike an opponent or a punching bag with a bare fist, the bones and soft tissues in your hand compress and absorb some of the energy of impact. If your hand is compressed and stable before impact, then it suffers less local tissue damage, and there are fewer broken bones in the hand. Hand wraps—and proper technique—are incredibly effective in reducing the likelihood of hand injuries, particularly broken bones. The term "boxer's fracture," where the fourth or fifth metacarpal bone is broken near the knuckle, has now become a misnomer, and many doctors prefer the term "brawler's fracture" because professional fighters seldom get them today.

When "Tank" Abbott chose to wear gloves in the octagon, it was not because he was concerned for the safety of his opponents. After knocking out John Matua in 1995, Abbott continued punching him as he lay unconscious on the mat, and then mocked Matua's involuntary muscle twitches after the referee pulled Abbott away. This was quite possibly the least sportsmanlike conduct in the history of MMA. Abbott's only concern was to protect his own hands from getting crushed against someone else's skull every time he threw a punch.

The feeling of "invincible hands" also allows fighters to punch each other much harder than they could with bare knuckles. This difference is more pronounced for larger fighters, and for unforgiving targets like the forehead, where bare knuckles are especially vulnerable to injury. In order to make their hands more resilient, some traditional martial artists train their fists on canvas bags or on *makiwara*, but even resilient hands can punch harder with gloves on. The best way to get a feel for the significance of this effect is to try it out at home. Strike a punching bag with your bare fists, and then with gloved (and wrapped) fists, and note how hard you are comfortable throwing your punches without injury. Have a friend hold up a book or a block of wood against the punching bag to get a feel for how much greater the difference is for hard targets.

Conclusion: Hand wraps provide protection from broken bones in the hand, but at the same time, "invincible hands" means a fighter can put much more effective mass behind the punch, increasing the momentum transfer and risk of diffuse axonal injury.

Greater fist weight increases mass but reduces speed.

Your fist, if you chopped it off at the wrist, weighs about a pound (16 ounces). An MMA glove might weigh about 4 ounces including the hand wraps, and a boxing glove might weigh between 10 and 16 ounces. This means you can double the mass of your fist by putting on a glove. If punching were as simple as throwing your fist at your opponent, we would expect double the mass to result in half the speed, but punches are complex actions involving much more of the body than just the fist.

In order to better understand the effect of gloves on punch speed, I performed a simple experiment, and I encourage you to perform the same experiment at home using your own technique and your own gloves. First I recorded myself punching without gloves as fast as possible (without sacrificing technique) for fifteen seconds, and then watched the video frame by frame and counted the punches. I repeated the process for MMA gloves (4.5 ounces) and then for boxing gloves (15.5 ounces). I evaluated three different punching techniques in order to get an idea for the full spectrum of the effect of glove weight on punches.

First I tested wing chun–style "chain punches," which involve a square stance, relaxed shoulders, and a vertical fist down the center. Almost all of the action for these punches comes from the arm, and the emphasis is on speed, rather than putting a large effective mass behind the punch. My punch speed started at 7.2 punches per second, dropped to 6.5 with MMA gloves (9 percent reduction in speed), and then dropped to 5.1 with boxing gloves (30 percent reduction in speed).

I also tested "brawler" punches, which involve a square stance and planted feet, but almost all of the motion comes from the shoulders and turning the torso, with very little flexing and extending of the arm. These are horizontal punches and they come in from either side, almost like alternating hooks. My punch speed started at 4 punches per second and remained unchanged with the addition of MMA gloves or boxing gloves (actually, it went up to 4.2, but this is possibly just a random fluctuation). I was able to maintain a steady rate of punching because the motion behind this type of punch is all torso and shoulder movement, rather than arm movement, and adding a few ounces to your body weight is negligible.

The last set of punches I tested was the jab-cross combination from a boxing stance, which involves arm extension, hip and shoulder rotation, and pushing off the back foot. This took the longest time between punches, at 2.9 punches per second, but it also showed no change with the addition of gloves (there was an increase to 3.3, but this is possibly a random fluctuation as well). Even though these punches involve extension of the arm, the execution of the punch involves the entire body, and a few ounces on the fists are not enough to slow down the whole process.

Of course, "punches per second" is not the same thing as "miles per hour," but since my arms were in constant motion during the chain punches, it is reasonable to assume that when I threw 30 percent fewer punches, it was because my fists were traveling 30 percent slower. It might be the case that my fists were traveling 30 percent slower during the jab-cross combination with the gloves as well, but because the twisting of my body took so long, the number of punches per second remained unchanged. Either way, the weight of the gloves reduced the speed of my arm movements, but it did not impact the movements of my body.

Conclusion: The added weight from wearing gloves may provide some small increase in momentum, but this effect is negligible

Punch speed as a function of glove weight

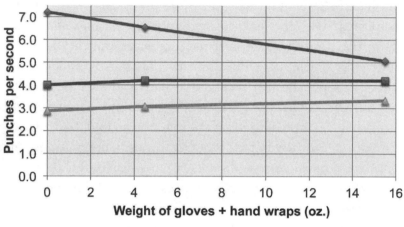

Figure 6-4. Punch speed as a function of glove weight. Punches that involve putting your body mass into the motion are not affected by glove weight. Chain punches, which primarily involve the arms, saw a speed reduction of 30 percent.

for strikes involving body mass. The added weight also significantly reduces the speed of the arm, but not for motions involving the whole body. This will make high-energy strikes more difficult, but high-momentum strikes will be unaffected.

When we put it all together, we get an unfortunate tradeoff.

Boxing gloves and MMA gloves are effective at absorbing and dispersing the energy of impact, which causes local tissue damage, but we have no reason to believe any gloves reduce momentum transfer. In fact, thanks to the excellent hand protection gloves provide, fighters are able to punch with greater momentum than they would with bare knuckles, and they are able to attack hard targets like the head more often. This means gloves do a great job of reducing the types of injuries associated with structural tissue damage (cuts, bruises, swelling, black eyes, and broken bones), but they also lead to an increase in the frequency and intensity of momentum transfer to the brain, which is directly related to diffuse axonal injury and CTE.

Fifty years ago, before we had a firm understanding of CTE, the choice was clear: use padded gloves to prevent injury. Today we need to think a little harder. A cut, a broken hand, or an eye injury might stop a fight or even end a fighter's career, but brain injury can take away a fighter's ability to function as a human being, both in and out of the ring.

CHAPTER 7

Brain Damage—Do Helmets Even Help?

As of the writing of this book, the National Football League is facing a $765 million lawsuit filed on behalf of more than 4,500 former players regarding the concussions and potential CTE sustained during their careers. Similar lawsuits are underway against the National Collegiate Athletic Association as well as the National Hockey League, and football helmet maker Riddell recently faced lawsuits over claims about the effectiveness of its helmets in protecting athletes from concussions. It seems CTE and headgear are important topics to athletes in a large number of sports, so for the purposes of this chapter, we will expand our scope beyond the world of martial arts and investigate the ability of various helmet types to protect us from diffuse axonal injury, which eventually leads to CTE. We learned in chapter 6 that boxing gloves provide us with protection from superficial injuries but they simultaneously increase opportunities for diffuse axonal injury. If we want to understand how headgear protects us (or doesn't), we will need to

Figure 7-1. Muay Thai/boxing headgear, baseball helmet, football helmet, and the human skull.

take a similar look into the physics behind the rotational motion of the human head with and without helmets.

Helmets are great at preventing skull fractures.

Almost all headgear, no matter what sport you play, is composed of a hard shell and a soft, compressible lining. The soft materials compress on impact, absorbing some of the energy of the blow, while the hard materials spread the impact energy over the surface of the shell, effectively increasing the surface area. We saw these same two principles at work during our examination of boxing gloves, and we saw there was no difference in momentum transfer, but the gloves were able to absorb and disperse some of the energy of impact. Since diffuse axonal injury is a result of momentum transfer to the brain, neither a hard shell nor a foam lining reduces the likelihood of CTE, but that does not mean these helmets are useless. Rigid shells and compressible materials are still very effective at protecting us from the types of injuries we tend to associate with localized tissue damage. This means they reduce the number of cuts, broken bones, bruises, "cauliflower ears," and other localized trauma. This also includes skull fractures, which should be considered a serious injury, even if the brain is not damaged with it.

In 1974 the National Operating Committee on Standards for Athletic Equipment (NOCSAE) defined its safety standards for helmets using a "linear drop test" (Gwin, Chu, Diamond, Halstead, Crisco, & Greenwald, 2010). The test, which the NOCSAE designed to prevent skull fractures and not CTE, involves dropping a head form with a helmet onto an anvil from various orientations. These standards have remained largely unchanged for more than forty years, and while there is ample evidence to believe the helmets that meet these standards reduce the likelihood of skull fractures, we have very little reason to believe they are effective at reducing the incidence of concussions or CTE.

Protecting from CTE means reducing angular motion of the head.

If we want to evaluate helmets on their ability to protect us from diffuse axonal injury, and ultimately CTE, we need to do some calculations to determine the angular velocity of the head immediately following impact. This will tell us how quickly the impact and all the applied forces got the head turning, which should be proportional to the magnitude of the stretching of axons in the brain.

MATH BOX

Angular Velocity of the Head

No matter what shape the force curve takes, and no matter what the angular acceleration profile looks like, a helmet's ability to protect you from diffuse axonal injury boils down to reducing the final angular velocity of your head, ω_{head}, following impact. In order to calculate ω_{head}, let's start with the momentum transferred to your head on impact, ρ_{impact}. For our purposes, we will assume ρ_{impact} is a constant we have no control over, since it is coming directly from your opponent. If we know how far the impact is from the center of rotation, R_{impact}, as well as the direction of the incoming momentum and the axis of rotation, we can calculate the angular momentum generated on impact, L_{impact}:

$$L_{impact} = R_{impact} \times \rho_{impact}$$

(continued)

where the "×" is the cross product, which accounts for both the magnitude and direction of the impact. You can also express L_{impact} in terms of angular velocity, ω_{head}, and the moment of inertia, I_{head}:

$$L_{impact} = \omega_{head} I_{head}$$

where I_{head} is the rotational equivalent of mass, defined as the sum of the mass of each little particle in the head, m_{head}, times the distance of that particle from the axis of rotation, r_{head}, squared. If we combine these equations, solving for ω_{head}, and allowing I_{head} to include both the head and the helmet, we get the following:

$$\omega_{head} = \frac{R_{impact} \times p_{impact}}{\Sigma m_{head} r_{head}^2 + \Sigma m_{helmet} r_{helmet}^2}$$

Looking at the equation for ω_{head}, we can see that heavier helmets do a better job of protecting our brains (m_{head} is on the bottom), but helmets that extend too far increase the risk of diffuse axonal injury (R_{impact} is on the top).

While there is some experimental evidence to imply the severity of diffuse axonal injury is different for each of the three rotational directions (Meany, et al., 1995), we will treat all angles of rotation equally here. Additionally, we will not make any attempt to specify the threshold at which significant diffuse axonal injury occurs. Instead, we will compare the results of each helmet to the human skull, and note the percent difference in final ω_{head}. Whether or not these percent differences are large enough or accurate enough to bring the severity and frequency of diffuse axonal injury below the threshold for developing CTE will require judgment and experimentation beyond the scope of our investigation.

"Helmet" #1: The Human Skull

The human skull is my favorite helmet of all time. It is rounded and rigid, and it does an excellent job of dispersing impact energy. There are even special sensors embedded in the skin to warn us when we are approaching the limits of what the skull can protect us from. The human head weighs about 9.65 pounds (Walker, Harris, & Pontius, 1973), and the center of mass of the head is just above and in front of the ear, and right between the eyebrows (Roush, 2010). The center of rotation of the head lies at the base of the skull, where the head meets the neck. For this chapter we will use my head as our sample of one, and it happens to be shaped like an ellipsoid, 6.5 inches from ear to ear, and 7.5 inches from front to back.

For these evaluations we will be making a number of over-simplified assumptions about the shape and mass distribution of

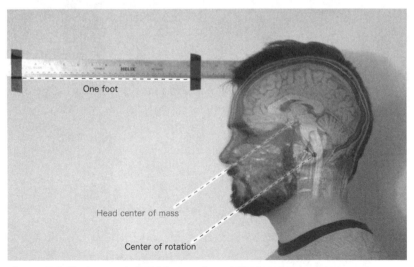

Figure 7-2. The human skull. This is actually an MRI of my head superimposed on a profile view of my head, so the location of the brain relative to the head is accurate. There is a 20 percent scale difference between the reference ruler and my head as a result of the depth of field.

heads and helmets, so you should consider the results to be rough approximations at best. For example, in my calculations I will approximate my head as a 10-pound cylinder of evenly distributed meat and bone with a radius of 3.5 inches. There are much more accurate ways to determine the magnitude of the diffuse axonal injury, such as "SIMon," a finite-element computational model that can determine the sheer forces experienced within the brain (Takhounts, et al., 2008). We will not attempt that level of accuracy, and we will focus instead on extracting relationships from the variables involved so we can determine what makes a good or bad helmet when it comes to protecting us from CTE.

MATH BOX

Angular Velocity Calculated, No Helmet

The cylindrical head approximation lets us use a formula instead of a summation for I_{head}, giving us the following equation for ω_{head}:

$$\omega_{head} = \frac{R_{impact} \times p_{impact}}{0.5mr^2} = \frac{R_{impact} \times p_{impact}}{61.25}$$

where R_{impact} could be 5.5 inches for a blow to the chin, 4.8 inches for a blow to the front of the face, 5.4 inches for the side and top of the head, or 5.8 inches for the forehead.

Helmet #2: Boxing / Muay Thai Headgear

I have a lot of experience with this gear, and I have fought a few bouts both with and without it. The loss of peripheral vision is annoying, and your head becomes a slightly larger target, but you may feel less dizzy after taking a few hits. It is made from stiff foam with a rigid frame, weighs 1 pound, and the center of mass of the helmet is just in front of the ear.

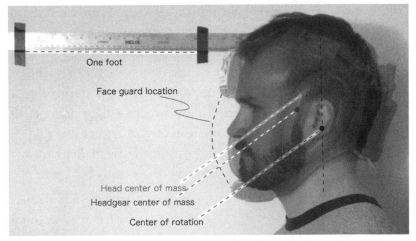

Figure 7-3. Boxing/muay Thai headgear, made primarily from rigid foam covering the sides and top of the face. This headgear did not come with a face guard, but I have drawn in the location of a hypothetical face guard for reference.

MATH BOX

Angular Velocity Calculated, Boxing/Muay Thai Headgear

The mass of the headgear is located on the front, side, and back of the head, which means a cylindrical shell with a mass of 1 pound and a radius of 3.75 inches is a sufficient approximation for the moment of inertia for this headgear:

$$\omega_{head} = \frac{R_{impact} \times P_{impact}}{I_{head} + I_{helmet}}$$

$$= \frac{R_{impact} \times P_{impact}}{0.5 m_{head} r_{head}^2 + m_{helmet} r_{helmet}^2} = \frac{R_{impact} \times P_{impact}}{75.3125}$$

where R_{impact} would be 4.8 inches for the face and 5.4 inches for the side and top (the same as the skull), 6.4 inches to the chin, and 7.0 inches to the forehead. An optional face cage would increase the face impact distance to at least 6.7 inches.

The additional weight (distributed in the front and back) reduces ω_{head} by 19 percent for blows to the face, side, and top of the head, but for the forehead and the chin, the impact distance is higher, which makes the reduction in ω_{head} less significant at 5 percent for the chin and 2 percent for the forehead. Even though this does provide some protection—you can feel the difference—these percentages still seem relatively low, given our expectations when we put on safety gear. In addition, if wearing this headgear makes a fighter more likely to train harder, the net effect could easily be negative.

I would like to take a moment, however, to address a particular style of fighting headgear with a face guard on the front, often advocated for children. It feels "safer" because you put your child's face behind a cage, where nothing can get to it, but in reality, the additional leverage from the cage puts your child at much greater risk for diffuse axonal injury. In fact, a hook to the face cage (a relatively easy target) will put 14 percent more stress on the axons in your child's brain than the same punch to the face without any headgear at all.

Helmet #3: Baseball Helmet

There are currently no class-action lawsuits against Major League Baseball for CTE on behalf of retired athletes, and baseball players tend to suffer fewer impacts to the head as compared to other athletes, but that does not mean baseball is without CTE risk as well. Ryan Freel was an aggressive, uninhibited player who sustained "nine or ten" concussions by his own count, and committed suicide in 2012, three years after his retirement from baseball. Researchers at the Boston University CTE center determined postmortem that Freel had been suffering from CTE. For aggressive players like Freel, a baseball helmet's ability to protect from CTE might not be a relevant metric because a large number of collisions with other players, walls, or the ground occur when the player is not wearing any helmet at all. We will still examine the effectiveness of baseball helmets in reducing diffuse axonal injury here, but we should keep in mind

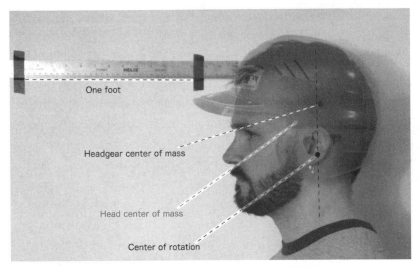

One foot

Headgear center of mass

Head center of mass

Center of rotation

Figure 7-4. A Baseball helmet, made from hard plastic and rigid foam, covering the top and back of the head only. I ordered a pink one because it was the least expensive, so don't judge me based on my choice of helmet colors.

MATH BOX

Angular Velocity Calculated, Baseball Helmet

The mass of the helmet is 1.3 pounds, and the mass is somewhat distributed in a semispherical orientation, which lets us approximate I_{helmet} with the equation for a spherical shell:

$$\omega_{head} = \frac{R_{impact} \times p_{impact}}{I_{head} + I_{helmet}}$$

$$= \frac{R_{impact} \times p_{impact}}{0.5m_{head}r_{head}^2 + \frac{2}{5}m_{helmet}\frac{r_{helmet}^5 - r_{head}^5}{r_{helmet}^3 - r_{head}^3}} = \frac{R_{impact} \times p_{impact}}{74.2728}$$

where R_{impact} would be 4.8 inches for the face and 5.5 inches for the chin (the same as the skull), 6.9 inches to the forehead, and 6.8 inches to the side and top of the head. Additionally, an impact that occurs at the tip of the rigid brim would have an impact distance of 7.9 inches.

these results may be only marginally meaningful when it comes to protecting the players overall.

The extra weight of a baseball helmet is helpful, so if you take a blow to the face or chin, it will reduce ω_{head} by 18 percent, but the added impact distance cancels out most of that benefit, resulting in only a 2 percent reduction for blows to the forehead and a 4 percent increase for blows to the side or top of the head. If you are unlucky enough to take a blow near the tip of the brim (in such a way that the helmet does not immediately pop off), the leverage provided will actually increase ω_{head} by 12 percent when compared to the forehead without a helmet. Even though CTE is not a primary concern for baseball, it seems the rigid brim is not worth the increased likelihood of injury, since a flexible brim would work just as well to block out the sun. From time to time rigid appendages such as ears, horns, or visors will appear on skate and snowboarding helmets, and I recommend you avoid them whenever possible.

Compared to all the other headgear we have looked at, football helmets are huge. They are heavy, which is good, but they also have a large radius, which provides a great deal of leverage for stretching axons.

The extra weight of the helmet manages to overcome the increased impact distance, marginally, so the helmet reduces ω_{head} by 14 percent for a blow to the forehead and 11 percent from the top side of the head, but the face guard extends much farther than the face without a helmet, resulting in a 2 percent increase in ω_{head} compared to the face without a helmet at all.

Of course, I have generated all these numbers using very broad assumptions, but I took this approach intentionally because it helps us see what factors go into a good (or bad) helmet better than a superaccurate simulation would. Fortunately, scientists at the Cleveland Clinic have conducted a very interesting and accurate investigation into football helmets, where they subjected crash-test dummies wearing helmets to various impacts, and then analyzed

Helmet #4: Football Helmet

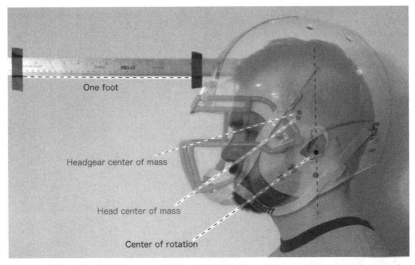

One foot

Headgear center of mass

Head center of mass

Center of rotation

Figure 7-5. A football helmet, made from hard plastic and foam, equipped with a metal face guard as well. The helmet pictured here is a youth large. The adult sizes are even bigger.

MATH BOX

MATH BOX: Angular Velocity Calculated, Football Helmet (Adult)

The mass of the helmet is 4.0 pounds, with a radius of 6.25 inches. The mass is somewhat distributed in a semispherical orientation, so we can approximate I_{helmet} with the equation for a spherical shell:

$$\omega_{head} = \frac{R_{impact} \times \rho_{impact}}{I_{head} + I_{helmet}}$$

$$= \frac{R_{impact} \times \rho_{impact}}{0.5 m_{head} r_{head}^2 + \frac{2}{5} m_{helmet} \frac{r_{helmet}^5 - r_{head}^5}{r_{helmet}^3 - r_{head}^3}} = \frac{R_{impact} \times \rho_{impact}}{132.9}$$

where R_{impact} would be 10.6 inches for the face, 10.8 inches to the forehead, and 10.4 inches to the side and top of the head. For reference, the youth helmet weighed 3.6 pounds, with a radius of 4.7 inches.

the results of the impacts with the SIMon computational model to determine the amount of diffuse axonal injury sustained (Bartsch, Benzel, Miele, & Prakash, 2012). The test compared 11 different modern helmets and two replica "leatherhead" helmets similar to those worn in the early twentieth century. The leatherhead helmets performed comparable to or better than modern helmets in all cases, which is consistent with the results I generated here using very broad assumptions.

The "invincible head" is a bug, not a feature.

One of the effects of absorbing and dispersing impact energy is an impaired ability to trigger the nociceptors in the skin that normally send warning signals to the brain, which are then interpreted as pain. This means an athlete can only feel prohibitive pain under a helmet in extreme cases. Pain is our internal warning system and it keeps us safe from serious damage by changing our behavior in the moment, and by teaching us lessons to remember for later. It is OK to turn off this warning system to avoid false alarms, like when we use a local anesthetic before surgery, because our warning system is not sophisticated enough to understand the difference between a life-saving surgery and a life-ending injury. When athletes put on helmets today, they are effectively switching off the warning system in their skull, but they are not switching it off to avoid false alarms. They are switching it off to avoid warnings of the very real damage their brains are suffering, and this allows them (and perhaps even encourages them) to take even harder hits without the inhibitions of pain.

Like American football, rugby and Australian-rules football are both high-collision sports, but athletes in neither sport wear helmets. Currently, we do not track and report brain injuries well enough to perform a meaningful risk comparison across all three sports, and rule differences make it difficult to isolate the effects of headgear, so it is impossible to say which sport is "safer," but once our head-monitoring technology improves a little bit, it might be worth testing whether taking football helmets off entirely would result in a safer game. Even if we are not ready to change the way we play the game on the field, taking the helmets off during practice might be a good start.

Physics can help us get head protection right.

Full disclosure: The following approach to the prevention of diffuse axonal injury, and ultimately CTE, is the subject of a patent application I have filed (application number 62/013,040).

If we want to construct a helmet that is effective at protecting an athlete from CTE, we need to pay close attention to the factors that make some helmets better or worse in the investigation above, and then put those factors to work for us. First we should notice that a slim form factor is important. The tighter to the skull we can keep the helmet, the better. The R_{impact} really hurts the performance of the majority of helmets we investigated. The second important factor is the mass. Increasing the mass of the head without significantly increasing the impact distance would be a great way to protect the head from diffuse axonal injury. In fact, we could make a simple protective helmet from a couple of aerobic wrist weights by sewing them together into a 5-pound beanie cap half an inch thick. We would need to add a strap to keep it tight to our heads, but this simple DIY project would reduce the ω_{head} in our calculations by 51 to 53 percent. This cheap design alone may be enough to save the brains of our athletes, and that is without doing any engineering to get it just right.

There is a second way to effectively add mass to the head as well. A martial artist is able to get a significant percentage of his body weight behind a punch by coordinating movement and becoming stiff at just the right moment. If we want to increase the effective mass of the head so much that we can reduce ω_{head} far below injury thresholds, all we need to do is connect the head to the body. We can do this via a rigid connection (perhaps something with sensors that becomes rigid on contact), or it could be a semirigid combination of compressible and stretchable materials and supports, like a second, supportive spine along the back of your neck. You can also think of it as providing a resistive force counter to the force applied at impact, but I prefer to think of it as borrowing mass. In any case, if we could get 10 percent of the body weight of a 200-pound athlete into the support of the head, which should be possible with minimal support connecting the head to the body, then we could reduce ω_{head} by 67 percent. Putting this together with the beanie cap above would result in a reduction of ω_{head} by more than 75 percent. If we start to put more than 10 percent body weight into the support (100 percent body weight means a completely rigid support), we may even begin to see the center of rotation shift away from the head and into the torso, where there is no potential for diffuse axonal injury.

The point is the helmets and headgear we use today are not doing enough to protect us from CTE, but it is possible for us to get it right and start protecting our athletes.

Bobbleheads require special consideration.

While the data we have today on concussions and brain injuries is insufficient for us to make meaningful comparisons across sports, it does seem as though women are more susceptible to concussions than men when engaging in similar activities. If this trend is real, and not an artifact of our reporting, it might mean that the thicker necks relative to head mass for male athletes allow them to borrow more mass from their bodies, similar to the method I proposed above. This implies athletes who work out their neck muscles might be able to lower the risk of brain injury. On the other end of the spectrum, young children, who are essentially built like little bobbleheads, may be at increased risk for brain injury, and we may want to develop special headgear just for them, with a focus on borrowing mass from the body instead of adding mass to the head.

Gloves and headgear in summary

Now that we have covered gloves and headgear across a variety of sports, and I have introduced a new approach to protect us from CTE in the future, I will bring the scope of our discussion back to martial arts and lay out a summary of gear available today, so you can decide for yourself what to wear when you train or fight.

Provides protection from:	Bare fists	MMA gloves	Boxing gloves	No headgear	Boxing headgear	With face guard
Hand injuries/fractures		X	X		X	
Cuts/bruises/black eyes		X	X		X	X
Eye gouges			X			X
Concussions/CTE					?	
Increases risk of:						
Hand injuries/fractures						X
Cuts/bruises/black eyes						
Eye gouges		?				
Concussions/CTE		X	X		?	X

Table 7-1. Glove and headgear options for martial artists evaluated for safety.

The sad truth is there are no good options available to us today. Ideally, we would use bare fists in combination with soft headgear that protects our eyes and our brains in a meaningful way, but for now, no matter what you choose, you will need to be careful.

CHAPTER 8

Guns, Knives, and the Hollywood Death Sentence

In order to become a successful screenwriter in Hollywood, you need to watch a lot of movies so you can learn from the screenwriters who came before you, and so you can get a feel for what else is out there and popular today. Unfortunately, this important part of a screenwriter's education is also how Hollywood ends up propagating and recycling incredibly stupid ideas over and over again to the point where the audience just accepts them without question. One such horrible inaccuracy occurs when a character is knocked out by a single punch and then wakes up in a different location. If you asked a competitive martial artist, he would probably tell you the most likely result of a knockout punch is only a few seconds of unconsciousness, and if you asked a football player, he may be able to share stories about teammates who lost consciousness for a few minutes or more, but if a character has been knocked out long enough to wake up in the next scene, that scene should probably take place in a hospital, and the rest of the movie should

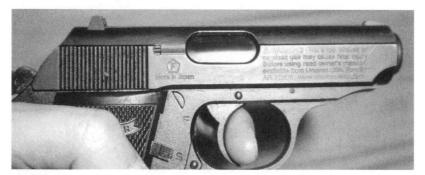

Figure 8-1. This is a BB gun. Shots fired from this gun can break the skin, but you probably won't need to call an ambulance.

probably be devoted to that character's very slow (and only partial) recovery from traumatic brain injury. These sorts of inaccuracies run rampant in Hollywood because everything a screenwriter knows about knockouts comes from watching some other screenwriter's characters get knocked out in the movies. For the most part, these sorts of inaccuracies end up being little more than comical bits of trivia, but when it comes to gun violence, a little Hollywood fiction can mean the difference between life and death in the real world.

Animals don't understand how guns work.

Hollywood gunshot wounds typically result in an instant death, where the victim grabs his chest and collapses to the floor, lifeless. This is, of course, nonsense. Unless the bullet has actually entered the brain, the only way someone is going to die from a gunshot wound (or from getting stabbed) is loss of oxygenated blood to the brain. This can happen as a result of bleeding out externally, bleeding internally, circulatory shock (inadequate levels of oxygen in tissues throughout the body), or cardiac tamponade (pressure from fluid in the sac enclosing the heart), but no matter what the specific process is, the basic premise is always the same: blood started flowing somewhere it was not supposed to be, and now there is not enough of it bringing oxygen to the brain. The time it takes for a person to die from these sorts of injuries can vary from a few seconds (for extreme cases, shotguns, assault weapons) to a few minutes to many hours. If it takes that long to die, why is it common for civilians to collapse to the ground immediately after getting shot in real life? Is there something more to a gunshot, or is it a case of life imitating art with potentially fatal consequences?

When a hunter shoots a deer, even if he shoots the deer right through the heart, he will still need to track that deer for another fifty to one hundred yards as it bleeds out and dies. Very rarely will an animal collapse immediately after getting shot. With the exception of a few cute and well-trained dogs, animals do not know they are supposed to play dead after being shot, so they run away instead. The effect is not limited to animals either. When the United States military fought against the Moro tribesmen of the Philippines in the early 1900s, the Moros earned a reputation as relentless warriors by continuing to fight uninhibited with their blades and spears, even after taking as many as fourteen gunshot wounds—much to the dismay of the American military men. This may be a somewhat exaggerated account, but the frightening conflict ultimately led to the US military increasing their handgun caliber from .35 to .45 in 1906, for additional "stopping power" (Boatman, 2005). It is unclear whether the Moros kept fighting out of sheer determination or firearm naïveté, but either way, they serve as an example of the human ability to keep going after being shot, until finally bleeding out.

It could be the case that humans tend to collapse from the pain of the shot, and to be fair, the prevailing expectation of a one-shot kill has been around longer than the motion picture industry, but I will still assert that the portrayal of gunshot wounds in Hollywood has helped to make this problem worse, not better.

Most gunshot wounds are survivable—but get help fast.

If we exclude suicides and accidental shootings from the statistics, your chances of dying once you have been shot during assault is somewhere around 20 percent (Gotsch, Annest, Mercy, & Ryan, 2001; Beaman, Annest, Mercy, Kresnow, & Pollock, 2000), but if we restrict ourselves to people who make it to the hospital alive, the number drops to 10 percent or less. This is incredibly important because these numbers are very far from certain death. If you get shot or stabbed during an assault, your odds of survival are still very good, but those odds depend heavily on how soon you can get medical attention (Fiedler, Jones, Miller, & Finley, 1986; Crandall, et al., 2013; Webb, 1999).

The necessity of prompt treatment is where Hollywood sets expectations that can become lethal inaccuracies. If a gunshot or stabbing victim believes he has just received a death sentence, and he collapses to the floor like in the movies, then it very well may become true. If, however, that victim knows a countdown clock started the moment he got shot, and speed of medical attention is the single most important factor in determining survival, perhaps more assault victims would find the ability to fight through the pain like Moro warriors and get to help.

Compliance with criminals is bad advice that comes from bad math.

Another unspoken Hollywood gun rule is the gamelike way in which the character holding a gun gets to make demands of the other characters, and they all have to do exactly what they are told. This can even become comical as the gun changes hands and characters take turns telling everyone else what to do. In real life, being held at gunpoint can be an unnerving experience, and your brain may not have a chance to orient itself enough to do anything but comply, but it turns out the unspoken rule of compliance depicted in the movies is a bad idea if you have an opportunity to take action.

Of course, we cannot lay all the blame on Hollywood. Prior to 1972 police reports were the only source for crime data, and those reports tended to show the trend that victims who resisted were more likely to get injured. This data was inadequate to get a full picture of crime, however, and it was nearly impossible to find remotely similar results when comparing data from city to city. As a result, the National Crime Victimization Survey (NCVS) was launched, and after years of side-by-side analysis of police reports and victim survey data, it became clear that police reports provided incomplete and poorly representative data (Block, 1981). The NCVS experienced a large overhaul in the 1980s to help improve the quality of the data, but it still looked like victims who resisted were more likely to be injured than those who complied. It was not until the second major overhaul in 1992, when the survey specifically asked victims if they started resisting *before or after* they were injured, that the real trend became clear. It turns out the correlation between resistance and injury (including sexual assault) was primarily due to cases where victims provided resistance only after they had been injured. If you correct this statistical error, victims who resisted their attacker were significantly less likely to be injured (Thompson, Simon, Saltzman, & Mercy, 1999; Tark & Kleck, 2004). In addition, 75 percent of the victims who resisted were of the opinion that their own actions improved their situation, while only 15 percent believed resisting resulted in greater injury.

Despite our relatively new understanding of the importance of resisting your attacker, the "conventional wisdom" about crime scenarios is still very prevalent. Law enforcement officers may tell you, "Don't be a hero," but you should keep in mind that the personal experiences of those officers focus very heavily on the small percentage of those victims who suffered greater injury as a result of their actions. In addition, the reason police departments and large corporations around the country adopt "Don't be a hero" as their official position might be because those institutions believe that position can protect them from liability in the event of a wrongful death lawsuit for millions of dollars.

Despite these outdated official positions, there are some scenarios where even "Don't be a hero" advocates will agree compliance is a bad idea. If an assailant ever demands you go to a secondary location, tie yourself up, or otherwise change the scenario to reduce the number of potential witnesses or make physical resistance impossible, this is because the assailant does not like his odds as they are right now, and he would like to put the odds more in his favor before proceeding. Your own odds will only get worse from this point on, so even if you don't think you have an opportunity, you need to resist or run.

Your best defense is the ancient art of run-fu.

Guns are great weapons for robberies and assaults because they can evoke the immediate fear of death, and the range allows the assailant to stay a safe distance from the fists and feet of his victims. This distance between the assailant and the victim also means the victim (hopefully) has the opportunity to turn around and run away as fast as possible. This may be a scary proposal, and it may be impossible if the victim is unable to come to his or her senses, is unwilling to leave a companion, or has been beaten, pepper sprayed, or cornered, but if it is at all possible to turn and run, the odds of survival are great.

If we look at your probability of dying and break it down into discreet conditional probabilities, we can put them together into an equation to help us understand how much you can improve our situation by running away:

$$P_{\text{death}} = P_{\text{shoot}} \cdot P_{\text{hit}} \cdot P_{\text{bleed out}}$$

where P_{death} is the total probability you die, P_{shoot} is the probability your assailant shoots at you (with the intention of hitting you) as you run away, P_{hit} is the probability he is successful in his attempt to hit you, and $P_{\text{bleed out}}$ is the probability that you die from the gunshot wound you receive. For each probability, we will pick a high-end and a low-end value, so when we multiply them all together, we can develop a reasonable range of final values for P_{death}.

$P_{\text{bleed out}}$ is probably somewhere around 20 percent, as we discussed earlier, but it could be as low as 10 percent if a victim has both the determination and the ability to get to medical help as soon as possible. We will pick a low-end estimate of 10 percent and a high-end estimate of 30 percent for this number.

P_{hit} is surprisingly low if your primary frame of reference is Hollywood. Trained police officers in action tend to hit their target only 43 percent of the time at distances less than 6 feet, or 23 percent for distances between 6 and 21 feet (Baker, 2007). When asked about their technique while firing in action, 61 percent of officers stated they were able to grip the gun with both hands, and 38 percent stated they were able to use their sights (New York City Police Department, 2013). Most criminals do not have the same quality of training as law enforcement officers, so it is safe to assume their percentages for using a two-handed grip or a gunsight will be lower, along with their chances of hitting the target. According to the Bureau of Justice Statistics' special report, *Weapon Use and Violent Crime*, only 27 percent of assaults where the assailant discharged a firearm resulted in the victim actually getting shot (Perkins, 2003). For this probability, we will pick a low-end value of 20 percent, and a high-end value of 40 percent.

P_{shoot} is the most difficult of the three probabilities to determine. If we consider only 15 percent of victims of assault who resisted their assailants felt their actions made the situation worse (Thompson, Simon, Saltzman, & Mercy, 1999), it would be unreasonable to assume a much higher percentage than this would open fire on a victim as he or she runs away, particularly when we consider that assailants wielding firearms are only half as likely to injure their victims as assailants wielding other weapons (or even no weapon at all) (Perkins, 2003; Thompson, Simon, Saltzman, & Mercy, 1999). Even though 15 percent is probably already too high, because of the uncertainty around this number, we will pick a low-end value of 10 percent, and a high-end value of 25 percent, just to err on the side of caution.

When we multiply these probabilities together, we get 25% * 40% * 30% = 3% for the high-end chance of dying, or 10% * 20% * 10% = 0.2% for the low-end chance. This is great news because it means if you turn and run, your chances of survival are somewhere between 97% and 99.8%. You will probably never see odds that good again if you comply with a stranger at gunpoint and get into his car.

Of course, the game changes considerably when you have friends or family with you. I recommend you have a conversation with your loved ones and ask them to run at the first sign of trouble, so you have already established that running away and getting help is the preferred plan of action, and not perceived as abandoning each other. You may also want to decide who should stay and who should run in an assault scenario, because sometimes you just don't have the option to run.

You are not fighting the gun; you are fighting the guy holding it.

For a few years I trained under an incredibly enthusiastic eskrima instructor who would occasionally give gun and knife defense seminars for law enforcement officials. One of the tricks he liked to pull started off with an offer to demonstrate how fast he was. He claimed he could run all the way across the gym and stab an officer with a rubber knife before the officer could draw his weapon (a rubber gun), aim it, and say "bang." Of course, nobody actually believed a little man in his late forties was going to shoot across the gym like a lightning bolt, but the officers played along. With a rubber knife in one hand, my instructor told the officer to draw as soon as he saw him charging, and then asked him if he was ready. Before he could respond, my instructor threw the knife at the officer, jogged partway across the gym while retrieving a second knife from his waistband, threw the second knife at the officer, jogged the rest of the way while retrieving a third knife from his waistband, and finally "stabbed" the officer with his third knife. The whole exercise may seem like cheating, but it is actually an effective demonstration of how to keep your opponent's mind preoccupied long enough to attack or get away.

It turns out the human brain is a pretty slow computer, and every time the scenario changes or something does not go as expected, the brain needs to take time to assess the situation and reorient itself. The processing time gets even worse when there are decisions to make, unknown factors come into play, or when the brain is under stress or otherwise impaired. In order to put things into perspective, when a human is asked to push a button in response to a light turning on (no decisions, no interpretations, just reaction), the response time is somewhere around 200 milliseconds (0.2 seconds), but that number can easily double when someone is asked to interpret a stimulus and choose an appropriate response (Kosinski, 2013). In one interesting study of reaction times (Blair, Pollock, Montague, Nichols, Curnutt, & Burns, 2011), researchers gave police officers and "suspects" handguns modified to fire wax bullets. The suspects kept their guns in their hands, with their arms extended down by their sides, the barrel pointing at the ground. The officers approached, drew their weapons, took aim at their suspect, and ordered him to put the weapon down. Prior to the experiment, some suspects had been instructed to comply, and others had been randomly chosen to respond by raising their weapon and firing at the officer. On average it took 380 milliseconds for the suspect to raise his gun, aim, and fire on the officer, but it took 390 milliseconds for the officer to process the situation, make the decision to shoot, and pull the trigger.

In chapter 6 we measured how many punches we can throw in a second, so if we invert those numbers, we get 139 milliseconds per punch for "arms only" chain punches, 250 milliseconds for "brawler" punches from the shoulders, and 349 milliseconds per punch for the jab-cross combo. These punches are all faster than the time it takes to interpret a stimulus and make a choice about how to respond, so how is it possible to block or dodge your opponent's punches during a regular sparing session if the fist travel time is less than your reaction time? The only reasonable answer is anticipation. You watch your opponent closely, you follow his eyes to anticipate his target, you wait for the slightest changes in distance and indications of movement in the neck and shoulders, and you learn his rhythm. This is one of the reasons many professional fighters start a fight by "feeling out" their opponents, and this is also one of the reasons a fight feels fundamentally different when you slow it down for the purposes of training. Feinting, where you start to throw a particular strike and then pull back or change to a different strike at the last moment, is particularly effective at full speed because of your opponent's reliance on anticipation. An opponent with a great poker face can be both effective and frustrating at full speed because there are fewer early warnings to follow. The reliance on anticipation is important because even though you may not be fast enough to dodge a bullet out of context, you are not fast enough to dodge a punch out of context either. You are, however, fast enough to anticipate an opponent's intentions, and act before he can reorient himself.

One of the reasons the "three knives" trick worked so well, besides lying to the officer and then forcing him to reevaluate the situation multiple times, is because it takes an incredibly large amount of brain processing time to determine if the parabolic arc of an object thrown toward you at moderate speed will hit you or not. To the best of my knowledge, there have been no studies done to quantify this effect, but anyone who played baseball as a child, or any sport where balls are thrown through the air, can provide some degree of anecdotal confirmation. The object doesn't need to be a knife, either, or even potentially deadly. Shoes, coins, rocks, drinks, phones, and car keys are just a few of a potentially endless list of useful items you could use to keep your opponent's brain preoccupied.

Of course, the power to keep your opponent's mind busy without giving it a chance to orient itself is not reserved for good guys only. Chances are if you have just been assaulted, robbed, or confronted, your brain will need some time to assess its own situation before you can even think about resisting or keeping your opponent's brain busy, and the stress or emotional state you are in will only make things worse. If your assailant uses this advantage effectively and intentionally, you may have very little opportunity to recover, but practice, scenario training, and an understanding of what is going on inside your own head can help you get past it and take action as soon as possible.

Guns and knives have levers built in for easy removal.

Intricate gun and knife disarming techniques can be fun to watch in the movies, but in a stressful situation, your best bet is to stick to the basics. For both gun and knife techniques, the first step is to try to get some measure of control over the hand. Ideally, you would grab the wrist, but you should consider any grab or pin of the arm a success because you don't get to be picky in these situations. At this point, if at all possible, you should try to bend your opponent's wrist. Again, this is not always an option, and time is of the essence, but if you can bend the wrist inward (outward also works to a lesser extent) you can greatly reduce your opponent's grip strength (O'Driscoll, Horii, Ness, Cahalan, Richards, & An, 1992). A fun way to test this out at home is to grab your left index finger with your right hand. Chances are your grip is strong enough to ensure you cannot pull your own finger out without first letting go. If you then bend your wrist inward as far as it will go, your left finger can slide out without very much resistance at all.

When it comes to guns, the barrel extends out from the handle and provides an excellent point of leverage, but in order to take advantage of this leverage, you need to ensure the fulcrum of the lever is located inside your opponent's hand so you are only fighting against your opponent's fingers, not his entire arm. You can do this by keeping the path of your own hand in a tight circle centered at the base of your opponent's thumb and index finger as you apply force to the barrel. Any direction is fine. If your circular path of motion is not centered near your opponent's thumb, you give your opponent the opportunity to resist your applied force with more than just his grip strength. For instance, if the fulcrum of the lever is at your opponent's wrist, he can resist by moving his hand, and if the fulcrum of your path is all the way back at your opponent's elbow, his forearm now provides more leverage than you have on the gun barrel and you will have a very difficult time disarming him.

Knives are slightly more difficult because you cannot grip the blade near the end to get lots of leverage without cutting your hand wide open or slipping off the end of the blade and losing control of the situation. For this reason you will need to apply force to one of the dull surfaces of the blade near the handle. Wrist control is much more important for disarming knives than guns. Some guys can pull off a single-handed gun disarming technique without ever even controlling the wrist. The fulcrum is the place where the base of the thumb and the index finger meet (the same

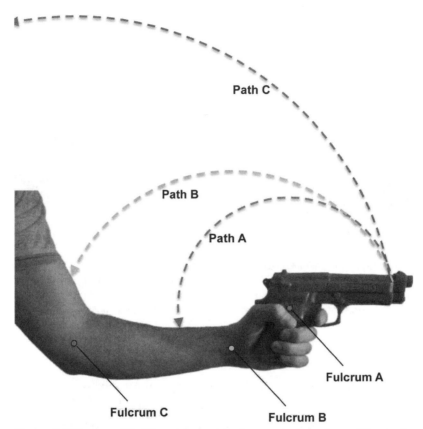

Figure 8-2. Three possible fulcrums for applying leverage in disarming, and the circular paths associated with each fulcrum. All paths are shown vertically here, but the same paths apply horizontally as well. **Fulcrum A:** The ideal disarming technique where your applied force has good leverage against your opponent's fingers. **Fulcrum B:** A less ideal (but not impossible) disarming technique where your opponent can counter your applied force with his wrist and grip strength. **Fulcrum C:** You will never get this gun.

fulcrum we used for the gun) whether your opponent is holding the knife with the blade up (saber grip) or the blade down (ice-pick grip). Because you have a little less leverage with a knife than you do with a gun, there are a few tricks to get a little extra force into your technique, such as a two-handed push/pull, a fast chop, bending the wrist inward, and snaking around your opponent's arm to get additional leverage off of his forearm.

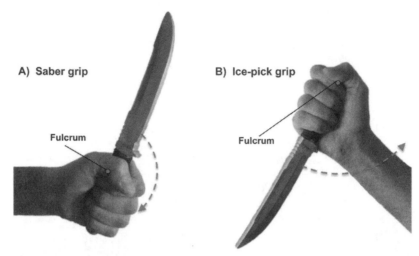

A) Saber grip

B) Ice-pick grip

Fulcrum

Fulcrum

Figure 8-3. Knife disarming technique fulcrums and paths. A) **Saber Grip:** The force is applied very close to the fulcrum in a tight circle. B) **Ice-pick Grip:** The force is applied farther away from the fulcrum, in a slightly larger circle. The ice-pick path is drawn in the forward/back direction for illustrative purposes here, but left/right is more effective because there is less overlap with the natural motion of the wrist.

Understanding the fulcrums and the paths for the knife and gun disarming techniques will help you learn them quickly, but if you don't practice them, the motions will feel foreign and they won't come together quickly enough to be effective. Try a few repetitions with a friend, using a toy gun, a stick, or a pen. Even if you never have to disarm an assailant with a knife, it may come in useful. I once peeled a spoon out of a baby's hand with perfect technique only moments before he could throw applesauce all over himself and the floor. Even though using martial arts to keep an unruly baby in check sounds like the very worst kind of made-up Hollywood garbage, moments like that will probably come up more often in your life than assault with a gun or knife.

CHAPTER 9

Qi and Pseudoscience in the Martial Arts

Qi (or *chi* or *ki*) is a prevalent concept in traditional martial arts, most notably in the East Asian styles, and some martial artists believe it is a source of power for strikes and submissions. We typically translate qi as a sort of "life energy," but it is not a scalar quantity like the scientific definition of energy, and a more complete definition of qi is fundamentally entangled within a much larger set of mystic beliefs. According to tradition, qi originates in your "dan tian," a special energy source located near your center of mass, and flows from the dan tian to the rest of the body along special channels called "meridians." Supposedly, if you apply pressure, needles, or strikes to specific locations, you can manipulate the qi in those meridians to either harm or heal a person. This explanation is, of course, a gross oversimplification of a very detailed and intricate tradition of medicine and martial arts (Yang, 1997), but it is a sufficient starting point for our investigation. We will begin by taking a look at some of the more outrageous claims of harnessing qi, and then work our way down to subtler claims, keeping in mind that if the impact of qi is so small that it is difficult to detect, the question of "Does qi exist?" then becomes "Do I even care if qi exists?" since harnessing its power would give you no measurable benefit.

Anecdotally, it appears that the number of martial arts instructors who include qi in their curricula has been dwindling over time, but because qi is so deeply rooted in traditional martial arts, even nonbelievers will still inform their students about it to give them a historical perspective of the art. We should give a lot of the credit for the waning appeals to mysticism in the martial arts to the UFC and other MMA promotions, which have risen in popularity over the last twenty years. As of the writing of this book, there have been exactly zero knockouts from "focused qi" inside the octagon. But the widespread incorporation of the internet into our daily lives and the convenience of recording video with a mobile phone deserve much of the credit as well. Today if someone were to witness a martial artist using a mystic force against an unwilling opponent, the witness could capture this astonishing event on video by simply pulling a phone out of his pocket. Given this very low bar we have for modern documentation of the supernatural, and given the potential for money and recognition, every year that passes makes the failure to validate the success of mystic forces like qi more and more damning.

The "no touch" knockout only works on your own students.

Perhaps the best-known public failure of mysticism in the martial arts occurred when National Geographic featured George Dillman on its 2005 special *Is It Real?* to test his claims that he could use qi to knock out an opponent without touching him. Dillman demonstrated the technique a number of times on his own students, and they all collapsed without difficulty. Dillman then appointed a practitioner, Leon Jay, to attempt a qi knockout on the pseudoscience investigator Luigi Garlaschelli. After multiple failed attempts on camera, Dillman attempted to explain the failure by pointing out Garlaschelli was a "nonbeliever" and adding that it is possible to "nullify" the technique by putting your tongue in the wrong place or by lifting both big toes.

Another one of Dillman's protégés, Tom Cameron, a.k.a. the "Human Stun Gun," suffered a similar embarrassment when Chicago Fox news reporter Danielle Serino took some Brazilian jiu-jitsu students to his school for an on-camera demonstration. Cameron masterfully demonstrated his qi knockouts on his own students, but when it came time to apply his skills to the Brazilian jiu-jitsu students, nothing happened. When asked to explain the failure, Cameron stated that only about 40 percent of people are susceptible to the technique and "natural athletes" are the toughest.

In Japan, Yanagi Ryuken, a *kiai* artist who was able to demonstrate his abilities on large numbers of his own students simultaneously, agreed to put his no-touch knockout to the test against an MMA fighter for cash in front of an audience, and at least two audience members recorded video of the event. At the beginning the MMA fighter waits as Ryuken waves his hands in the air. The fighter then approaches the old man unabated and punches him directly in the face, knocking him onto the floor, ass first. Ryuken grabs his mouth in shock and disbelief, and checks his hand for blood. The MMA fighter seems somewhat concerned for Ryuken's safety, but Ryuken recovers quickly, and the referee resets the fight. Again the MMA fighter walks right through Ryuken's imaginary defenses, grabs his sleeve, and showers him with punches as Ryuken cowers and collapses to the floor.

One interesting common thread to the proponents of no-touch knockouts above is they were all able to knock down their own students or believing participants, but as soon as a single resisting opponent appeared, all power was lost. Whether the willing participants were knocked out by qi or by hypnotic suggestion, the no-touch knockout is not a viable technique for use against an unwilling opponent, which makes it impractical for either sport or self-defense. If learning these techniques gives someone a false sense of confidence, as it did for Yanagi Ryuken, you could even argue that learning the art of the no-touch knockout actually places a person at greater risk in a self-defense scenario than learning nothing at all.

Qi demonstrations are usually just physics tricks.

Slightly less brazen than the claims of "knockout qi" are the demonstrations of how harnessing qi can supposedly give martial artists (or monks) the ability to perform amazing feats of strength and imperviousness. These demonstrations often include breaking concrete blocks, lying on a bed of nails, and walking on hot coals. Even though both the demonstrator and the audience may believe the explanation behind the impressive demonstration is qi, we can explain all such demonstrations with a little physics. For our purposes here, I will stick to demonstrations performed in earnest, and not magic tricks performed with intent to deceive the audience— but keep in mind the boundary between the two is not always clear.

The first time I ever saw someone lie on a bed of nails was when a team of motivational speakers came to my middle school to tell us to say no to drugs. The team was made up of bodybuilders dressed in colorful spandex, and they took turns performing a number of strongman tricks while their teammates flexed and yelled lines into the microphone: "He's never tried to lift that much weight before! Can he do it? This might be a new world record right here! Ooooooh! HE DID IT!" Even as a child, it was apparent to me that each of these men had dreams of becoming the next Hulk Hogan, but performing for a group of middle school students was the closest they would ever come to that dream. They performed such feats as brick breaking, board breaking, metal rod bending, and lying down sandwiched between two beds of nails while someone broke a cinder block on top of them with a sledgehammer. They explained to us that they were able to perform these amazing feats because they all refused to try drugs even once.

During my first year of college, a skinny gray-haired physics professor asked a student volunteer to lie down sandwiched between two beds of nails while the professor broke a cinder block on top of him with a sledgehammer. This was the exact same trick I had seen in middle school, except this time there were no spandex, no muscles, and I was pretty sure the student volunteer had tried drugs once or twice. A few years later, when I started grad school, the chair of the physics department performed a demonstration where he walked on hot coals, and when I started teaching lab classes, I even performed a few tricks myself. My personal favorite was sticking my bare hand into liquid nitrogen (at -321 degrees Fahrenheit). It turns out these sorts of tricks are the result of simple physics rather than spiritual strength, and because of the entertaining visuals, they have become standard demonstration tools for physics departments around the country.

In case you ever encounter someone trying to use physics tricks to justify mysticism, here is a handy guide to some of the most common ones, how they work, and a simple change you could make that would cause the trick to fail. Even though you already have the ability to perform any of these tricks without harnessing any qi at all, please keep in mind that you can always make a nonmystical mistake and hurt yourself, so I do not recommend trying any of these at home.

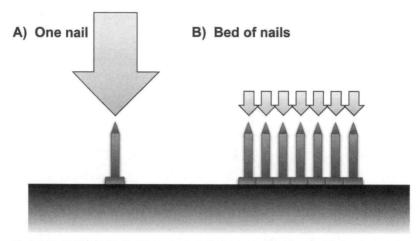

Figure 9-1. A) One Nail: All the applied force (pictured as an arrow) is focused on the tip of the nail, making it very dangerous and painful. **B) Bed of Nails:** The force is evenly distributed over each nail, making the force per nail much smaller.

Lying on a bed of nails

The trick: The performer shows he is impervious to injury by lying down on a bed of nails.

The physics: It hurts to sit on a nail because the surface area of a nail is very small, so the applied force (your weight) is all localized at the tip of the nail. If you sit on a hundred nails at the same time, the force is spread out evenly over each of the nails, making the force per nail only 1 percent of your body weight. Any person is capable of performing this trick right now with no training.

How to ruin it: Sit on a single nail by itself.

Lying on swords

The trick: The performer shows he is impervious to injury by lying down on the blades of multiple sharp swords.

The physics: This is similar to the bed-of-nails trick because lying across three blades provides more surface area than one, but there is another factor at work here unique to cutting squishy things like people. It turns out even if the blade is sharp, cutting compressible material like gelatin or human skin is difficult to do with evenly applied pressure because the material can compress as you apply pressure to it (Reyssat, Tallinen, Le Merrer, & Mahadevan, 2012). If you want to cut something compressible, you either need to use a slicing motion to run the imperfections of the blade along the surface, or you need to angle the blade (like a guillotine) so you can make the initial incision with a small surface area. A great household example of this is slicing bread. It is very difficult to just chop through a loaf of bread, but if you start at an angle and use a slicing motion, it is easy.

How to ruin it: Lie on a single sword, or put the swords at an angle instead of horizontally.

Breaking boards or bricks

The trick: The performer punches through boards or bricks using qi to generate immense power.

The physics: We tend to think of bricks and boards as very strong, but they are only strong when it comes to compressive strength. Compressive strength is great for supporting heavy structures, which is why we use these materials for construction, but when a performer breaks a board or a brick, he is not testing the compressive strength of the material. Instead, the performer is trying to generate a microscopic bend in the board or brick he is striking. If you take a bendy straw and bend it, you will notice the straw inside the bend is compressed, but the straw outside the bend is expanded. Cinder blocks and dry pine boards are strong when it comes to resisting the compression on the inside of the bend, but not nearly as strong when it comes to resisting the expansion on the outside of the bend. They are also very brittle, which means they cannot stretch to accommodate the bend, and they will break in half when bent even a small amount (Feld, McNair, & Wilk, 1979). When it comes to multiple breaks, performers will place

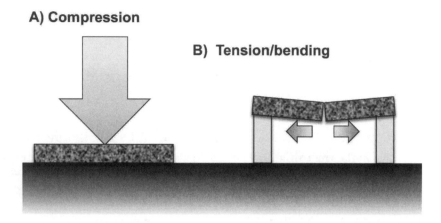

Figure 9-2. A) Compression: Wood, cinder blocks, and bricks are very strong when it comes to compressive forces. **B) Tension and Bending:** With only a small bend, the material on the far side begins to pull apart. Brittle materials are not strong with respect to these kinds of forces.

spacers between the boards or bricks, so there is very little change in the minimum force required for breaking multiple boards. Breaking two boards with spacers can be thought of as breaking one board twice. Almost anyone is capable of simple board and brick breaks with less than five minutes of instruction, although some exceptional practitioners have taken the skill to impressive extremes. Avoiding injury in the hand is partially the result of good punching technique, but conditioning the hand over time with exercises like makiwara training or punching canvas bags of rice can greatly increase the bone density in the hand, leaving it less susceptible to injury (Chen, Liu, You, & Simmons, 2010). Scientists are even investigating vibrational bone conditioning as a potential treatment for osteoporosis (Verschueren, et al., 2011).

How to ruin it: Try to break a single brick laid flat on the floor, instead of a stack of ten separated by spacers. Alternatively, move the spacers or supports closer together and closer to the point of impact.

Breaking long wooden beams with an "iron body"

The trick: One performer takes off his shirt, and a second performer swings a long wooden board, striking the shirtless performer on the stomach or back. The board breaks, but the performer is fine.

The physics: This trick is somewhat similar to board breaking because the wood used is brittle, and it can definitely help if you condition your body over time, but there are other factors at play here as well. One important factor is the length of the board. Longer boards can bend farther before they break, but they also take less force to break because of the additional leverage they provide. The other important factor is where the board strikes the performer. The board's center of mass is in the middle, but the point of impact with the shirtless performer is between the board-holding performer and the center of mass. While getting hit with a board hurts in any scenario, fighters can think of this like "crowding" a roundhouse kick or a haymaker. If you get close enough, it turns into more of a swift push than a big hit. Additionally, since the center of mass of the board is located beyond the point of contact, the mass of the board continues to travel in a circular path after impact, causing the board to bend around the shirtless performer instead of pushing into him. If the performer swinging the board holds on tightly, the board will break. Even though it would hurt and, again, conditioning helps, almost anyone is capable of being the shirtless performer in this scenario today.

How to ruin it: Try hitting the shirtless performer with the end of the long stick, or use a short stick instead.

Bending a spear or rod

The trick: The performer places the end of a spear or a long metal rod into his neck or stomach and then pushes forward, bending it instead of impaling himself.

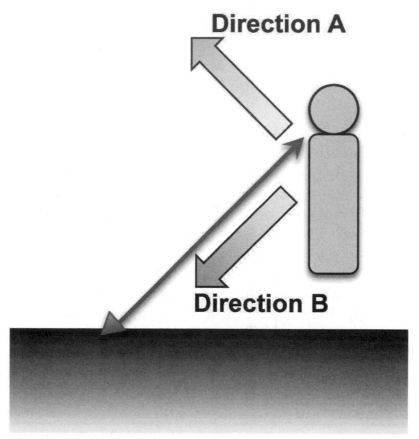

Figure 9-3. A spear is secured to the ground with the tip placed on the performer's neck. **Direction A:** Pushing in this direction will bend the spear without hurting the performer. **Direction B:** This will kill the performer.

The physics: Long, narrow objects like spears and metal rods are very strong along the direction of their length, but not very strong at all in the directions perpendicular to that length. Even though it may be difficult to see, the performer is not pushing his neck directly into the shaft of the spear, but at a 90-degree angle to the shaft, causing it to bend.

How to ruin it: Grease up the spearhead or rod so there is less friction available to control the direction of the applied force.

Licking a hot shovel / hand in hot lead / hand in liquid nitrogen

The trick: The performer licks a glowing hot metal shovel, or dips a hand in water and then sticks it into molten lead without getting burned. Scientists also love to perform similar tricks with super cold liquid nitrogen.

The physics: This trick is possible due to an interesting phenomenon called the Leidenfrost effect (Walker J., 2010), which occurs when a liquid comes into contact with a substance much hotter than its boiling point. If you stick your hand in water and then stick it in hot lead, the thin layer of water coating your hand will instantly turn into a gas, and the pressure from that gas keeps you safe by pushing the molten lead away from your hand. Licking a hot shovel works the same way, where the water in your saliva instantly turns into a gas, which keeps the hot shovel from ever actually coming into contact with your tongue. For liquid nitrogen tricks, the hand should be dry because the temperature is extremely cold (-321 degrees Fahrenheit), instead of hot. Your body heat boils the liquid nitrogen, which creates a small pocket of gas to insulate your hand from the cold liquid. This effect only lasts for a few moments, but it is still incredibly impressive to watch, even if you already know how it works.

How to ruin it: Dry off the hands/tongue for lead or hot shovels. Get the hands wet for liquid nitrogen.

Walking on hot coals

The trick: The performer shows he is impervious to burns by walking across hot coals.

The physics: This seems impressive because the coals are glowing red from the heat, but it turns out the coals are actually not very good at conducting heat, so the activity is not as treacherous as it appears. In addition, with every step one foot is cooling off in the air, which is why performers tend to use a brisk walk for this trick. It is possible that the Leidenfrost effect also contributes to the trick, since wet or sweaty feet seem to help, but it could also just be a case of water absorbing a lot of heat before it gets hot (Walker, J., 2010; Willey, 2010).

How to ruin it: Stand in place on hot coals.

This is by no means an exhaustive list of physics tricks used to justify belief in mystic powers, but hopefully it is enough for you to inoculate yourself against such demonstrations in the future. Considering people were performing these tricks long before we understood the science behind them, we can expect that the performers relied on mystical explanations. Now we have all the science we need to explain them—and much more—so there is no longer any excuse to pretend those tricks are the result of harnessing qi or saying no to drugs.

Qi has no measureable effect on your health.

The claim that you can use qi to improve health is possibly the least outlandish claim that could be made without stripping it of all meaningful connection to the physical world. This is a very difficult claim to test, but fortunately, scientists and doctors have performed a large number of medical studies with this very goal in mind. Despite a disturbing frequency of issues with individual trials, if you look at the results of many trials together, accounting for prevalent biases and poor quality, it becomes clear that no mystical therapies are capable of providing a meaningful or even detectable amount of improvement to your health.

In the 1970s the nurse Dolores Krieger and the mystic author Dora Kunz invented a purported energy healing method called "therapeutic touch," which involves placing hands near a patient to transfer energy to him and heal his "human energy field." Therapeutic touch gained popularity with nurses throughout the

1980s and 1990s, until a little girl named Emily Rosa decided to test one of its key principles for her fourth-grade science project. In 1996 and 1997 she ran a series of tests on therapeutic-touch practitioners of all levels, where she asked participants to stick both hands through a screen so they could use them to sense human energy fields, but they could not see anything beyond the screen. Rosa, sitting on the other side of the screen, then randomly selected one of the practitioners' hands and held her own hand out above it. If therapeutic touch practitioners possessed a genuine ability to sense human energy fields, they should have been able to guess which of their own hands was close to Rosa's hand with a probability better than random chance. On average the practitioners guessed correctly 44 percent of the time, indicating they were not capable of detecting a human energy field. With the help of some grown-up researchers, including her parents, at the age of eleven Emily became the youngest coauthor to publish a paper in the *Journal of the American Medical Association* (Rosa, Rosa, Sarner, & Barrett, 1998), and the popularity of therapeutic touch began to decline with the ensuing media coverage.

Reiki is a Japanese energy therapy, similar to therapeutic touch, where a trained practitioner places hands on or near a patient and allegedly transfers qi in order to heal him or her. Despite the decline of therapeutic touch, Reiki has managed to maintain some popularity, and as a result there have been a number of medical trials testing the health benefits of Reiki. When researchers pooled all these studies together into a systematic review, or a meta-analysis, it became clear that not only was there no measurable health benefit from performing Reiki, but also a large number of individual studies were at high risk for bias or showed other signs of poor execution or design (Lee, Pittler, & Ernst, Effects of Reiki in clinical practice: A systematic review of randomised clinical trials, 2008; VanderVaart, Gijsen, de Wildt, & Koren, 2009).

Traditional Chinese medicine includes acupuncture, a process where a practitioner places needles subdermally at special points on meridians to positively affect a patient's qi; Chinese herbal treatments, which involve ingesting substances thought to have positive effects on a person's qi; and *qigong*, a combination of internal and external practices where qi is employed to improve health. Investigations into the efficacy of these practices suffer the same quality and bias issues as Reiki and other "alternative" options. These issues make it nearly impossible to rely on the results of individual trials (Cao, Liu, & Lewith, 2010; Wang, Li, Liu, Luo, Ma, & Alraek, 2014), and even the systematic reviews have a high rate of biases and other issues (Ma, 2011).

It is understandable that we would see some bias in these scenarios because all of the trials require the involvement of someone who is personally committed to the mysticism being tested, but there is also a subtle yet important trend in the types of issues that appear in the trials and the reviews. One of the most common problems with trials is insufficient sample size, or testing too few patients to calculate the difference between the test and control groups. This is a ridiculous problem to have en masse, because calculating the minimum sample size is a simple task for anyone with statistical training, and it can even be done entirely over the phone. If a five-minute phone conversation is all it takes to make sure the money and time put into conducting a trial do not end up wasted on inconclusive results, then why has it become a recurring theme in trials of mystic claims? Personally, I don't believe the answer to this question is an epidemic of incompetence, intentional dishonesty, or poor planning. More likely, we are witnessing an epidemic of enthusiasm. When you calculate the minimum sample size for a trial, one of the numbers you need to include is your "estimated lift," or how much you think the test will outperform the control. If you were designing a test to prove how awesome your own brand of magic therapy is, you would have to answer the question, "What percent of patients do I expect to cure with my magic?" If you gave a very enthusiastic answer, like, "My magic will cure 75 percent of my patients," then the minimum sample size needed to measure your miracles might be fewer than 20 subjects. If your magic only cured less than 1 percent of your patients, you would probably need more than 20,000 participants, and you would also need to make sure you accounted for the placebo effect. Since neglecting to sufficiently control for the placebo effect is one of the other common problems with these studies, I think it is safe to assume the significant lack of quality in the research into traditional Chinese medicine and other mystic healing arts can be partially attributed to perpetual overenthusiasm from the researchers involved.

Acupuncture is by far the most popular form of traditional Chinese medicine in the United States, so it is not surprising to hear that is it also the most thoroughly tested. Despite the frequency of quality issues with studies, the systematic reviews either point to the need for more data and larger sample sizes or no measureable difference whatsoever (Vickers, et al., 2012; Madsen, Gøtzsche, & Hróbjartsson, 2009). To get around the placebo effect acupuncture researchers have even developed a number of clever techniques, called "sham acupuncture" (Park, White, Stevinson, Ernst, & James, 2002; Moffet, 2009), where a patient is tricked into believing he or she has just received acupuncture treatment. The irony of the name "sham acupuncture" is that it is just as effective as "real acupuncture," but without the false pretenses of qi (Colquhoun & Novella, 2013; Singh & Ernst, 2008).

Chinese herbal treatment trials tend to have the same bias and quality issues as acupuncture trials, and also come to the same results: inconclusive, with a larger sample size needed, or no measurable effect (Shang, Huwiler, Nartey, Jüni, & Egger, 2007; Liu, Zhang, He, Li, & Kang, 2006). Some Chinese herbs do have actual medical applications, such as artemisinin, which we use to fight malaria (Van Agtmael, Eggelte, & van Boxtel, 1999), but this is not its traditionally prescribed purpose, and finding an isolated medical use for an herb does not validate the concept of treating your health through your qi in general. Many Chinese herbs have no measurable effect, and some are even toxic, such as aristolochic acid, which was discovered to cause a type of kidney disease named Chinese herbs nephropathy (Cosyns, 2003).

Even though qigong relies heavily on the concept of qi, it is arguably the most difficult of the traditional Chinese medicine practices to test because the mysticism is deeply intertwined with a large number of activities that provide well-known nonmystical health benefits, such as stretching, relaxation, abdominal breathing, and low-impact exercise. Again, there are many trial (and review) quality issues, including bias and small sample size (Lee, Oh, & Ernst, Qigong for healthcare: An overview of systematic reviews, 2011), but the results for testing the mystical side of qigong mirror those of every other test for qi, resulting in larger samples needed, or no measurable benefit (Lee, Pittler, & Ernst, Internal qigong for pain conditions: A systematic review, 2009; Park, et al., 2013).

If the impact of qi is so small that it is undetectable without massive sample sizes, I will argue that it doesn't even matter if qi exists because it is useless. It cannot give you super powers, like the no-touch knockout, it is not the source of power for performing tricks, like breaking boards, and it is not even capable of improving your health by a small measureable amount. In fact, to the degree that people reject proper medical care in favor of qi, it may provide a negative health effect overall. It is difficult to document how often patents choose mysticism over medicine, but in 2003 Steve Jobs, Apple founder and CEO, learned he had a small tumor on his pancreas and declined surgery, against the recommendations of his doctors, family, and friends. Instead, he used a combination of acupuncture and herbal remedies for nine months, until finally agreeing to surgery, where the doctors discovered the cancer had spread to his liver (Isaacson, 2011). Jobs passed away in 2011 at age fifty-six as a result of this cancer. It is impossible to know what would have happened if he had made different choices for his treatment, and it is impossible to know how widespread the problem of treatment substitution is, but his story can help us understand that belief in mystic cures is definitely not harmless.

There is treasure buried in the trash.

Even if the underlying magic is fiction, qigong and *taiji* are enjoyable, relaxing, and low-impact exercises that can be very beneficial to your health. Harnessing your qi may not give you any special powers, but yelling when you strike is a great way to momentarily tighten the muscles in your abdomen and intimidate or distract your opponent. Just because the traditional explanation is nonsense, it doesn't necessarily mean a technique is ineffective. In some cases we may have developed a technique long before we had the science to explain it, and we invoked mysticism because human beings are not very good at saying "I don't know." Of course, systematic mysticism is also the ideal breeding ground for impractical garbage, but when it comes to fighting, I believe there is still some genuinely good content hidden alongside the garbage.

Pressure points are a great example of value hidden in mysticism. The explanations for why they work tend to be heavily rooted in qi and meridians, but I have personally (and unwillingly) dropped to my knees after a training partner shoved his thumb into a pressure point inside my elbow. Pressure points have the potential to be very powerful tools, but we will never know for sure until we can find the science hidden in the fiction. Which points are actually effective at controlling a resisting opponent? Why does a thumb inserted into the inside of the elbow hurt so much, really? Is it stretching or tearing tendons? Is it just pain, like pulling hair, or is it pain as an early warning of serious damage, like an arm bar? There is still significant work that needs to be done to ground these techniques in science, but we should not dismiss this area of martial arts merely because of its deep ties to mysticism.

CONCLUSION

You're Only Getting Started

"I think I can safely say that nobody understands quantum mechanics."

—Richard Feynman

This book is only one piece of the puzzle.

Even though I intended this book to be your unfair advantage in a fight, it is, by itself, incomplete. The knowledge and understanding you take away from these pages will help you learn faster while you train, get more out of your training, and better apply your training in a real, stressful situation, but all of that is meaningless if you don't train. There is a reason most undergraduate physics classes have labs as well as lectures: when you read something in a book, you might remember it, but when you apply what you have read in a hands-on scenario, you own it.

137

Traditional martial arts can benefit from science and sparring.

A profound statement can be difficult to distinguish from a painfully obvious one, particularly in hindsight, so it is not surprising to hear the most important lesson science has to offer martial arts is the need for realistically stress-testing your skills. While the majority of martial arts schools do include sparring, it is often with the assumption that your instructor provides wisdom to you, and sparring sessions serve as chances to validate your instructor's guidance. A more scientific approach (which sometimes appears in styles that train for competition) would be to view sparring as the source of wisdom, while your instructor's guidance merely provides you with the tools you need to better extract and interpret that wisdom.

Brazilian jiu-jitsu has earned a good reputation in mixed martial arts, and a large part of that success is a direct result of its scientific approach. By narrowing its scope to exclude many of the potential sources of serious injury (i.e., no punches or kicks), practitioners of Brazilian jiu-jitsu have the ability to provide genuine resistance during training, and gain a level of experience unattainable in other styles. In Brazilian jiu-jitsu it is common to train for contingent scenarios, like, "If you can control the arm, go for technique A, but if he won't let you get the arm, do technique B." It is also common to train techniques for situations where you have already screwed up and ended up in a bad position, such as escapes once you've been mounted. This approach to training comes from an appreciation for the chaotic nature of a fight, and it would not exist without personal stress-testing experience. Of course, not every style has the option of limiting the scope to the same extremes as Brazilian jiu-jitsu, but every style does have the option to take a pragmatic approach to martial knowledge and constantly learn and relearn what works and how things can go wrong.

You don't have to give up the art to embrace the science.

People practice martial arts for a number of different reasons. Some enjoy the sport and the competition, some want to be prepared for a self-defense scenario, and some desire fitness, self-improvement, discipline, or culture. Many practitioners celebrate the "art" in martial arts and would not want to lose that beauty to the sometimes harsh realities of science. While it is understandable to have an attachment to the beauty of martial arts in forms and techniques, the legitimacy behind the beauty, and the awe and respect that separate martial arts from pure performance art come directly from their efficacy in self-defense applications.

While a scientific approach may very well cleanse an art of numerous ineffective techniques, it will never take the beauty away from the practice. Science itself is a celebration of natural beauty, identifying the simple truths that help us make sense of a complex universe, and martial artists will find the natural beauty of their styles becoming even more polished and refined with the application of a little science. In addition, fighting will always be a complex chaos, and navigating that chaos will always be an art form.

A fight is chaos, so take lots of data.

A "fight" can mean a lot of very different things. It could be a sparring session with your training partners, a competition, a match in the ring, a full-on assault on the street, or even two young men with more testosterone than brains, vying for dominance in a bar. Depending on how much of a surprise the scenario is, your brain will need to take some time to orient itself, and your sympathetic nervous system may even start the fight-or-flight process by releasing a bunch of cortisol and epinephrine (adrenaline).

The brain-orientation and the fight-or-flight processes in combination can make you feel so different from when you're in a comfortable sparring session with your training partners that many professional and amateur fighters claim ring experience and training experience are two totally different things. Law enforcement officers and assault victims will often say the same about their experiences on the street.

The context of a fight can vary wildly as well. There are different rules, or levels of acceptable violence, different implied repercussions after the fight, different settings, different emotional states, and much more. It is very difficult to look at one fight and draw conclusions from that experience you can apply to all others. There are too many unknowns and too many different ways things can go wrong when the pressure is on for anyone to draw meaningful conclusions without a massive amount of actual ring or street experience.

Your mind and your body disagree on how much experience you need.

The primary challenge to becoming an expert fighter—and not just an expert practitioner or trainer—is in order to get the experience you need, you have to put your body (and life) at risk. In Malcolm Gladwell's book *Outliers: The Story of Success*, he examines exceptional people and tries to determine what was different about them that helped make them successful. One important and recurring contributor to success is a unique opportunity to amass a large amount of experience, and by his rough estimates, to become an expert at something to an outstanding degree, you need to get somewhere around ten thousand hours of experience (Gladwell, 2008). If you train in martial arts for three hours a week starting at age fifteen, without ever taking time off, this means you will have ten thousand hours of training experience after about sixty-four years, when you are seventy-nine years old. If you increase your training time to six hours a week, you can get there in thirty-two years, when you are forty-seven years old. Training is not the same as fighting in the ring or on the street, however, so if we assume (generously) that each fight lasts ten minutes (many fights don't even last sixty seconds), in order to get ten thousand hours' experience of actual ring or street experience, you need to have more than sixty thousand fights under your belt. This is, of course, an absurd number, because most professional fighters typically only fight a couple of times a year, and very few fighters have ever had more than one hundred fights in their career.

The reason fighters can never acquire enough experience to get anywhere close to ten thousand hours is that every minute they spend in the ring or training hard in the gym comes with a very high risk of injury. Many muay Thai champions retire from fighting and start teaching other fighters before they even turn thirty-five. The human body—and the brain—cannot recover from all the minor and major injuries they would sustain in order to reach ten thousand hours of expertise.

There are no experts on fighting or violence.

Ten thousand hours is not exactly a rigorously determined milestone, but if we don't like it, we can also look at fight experience statistically. For every unknown in a fight (and a fight is full of unknowns), we need enough unbiased encounters to develop a trend that doesn't accidentally mislead us because of one or two atypical cases. For example, if you wanted to know how often a fight goes to the ground, you would need to look at each fight in your experience and answer the question with a yes or a no. If you only have one fight in your experience, then your answer would be either 100 percent or 0 percent of all fights go to the ground. Having two fights means the only possible choices are 0 percent, 50 percent, or 100 percent, which is still horrible, but better than one fight. Generally speaking, statisticians tend to recommend at least thirty instances before a binary (yes/no) starts to look like a reasonable percentage, but personally, I don't feel confident generalizing on any less than fifty, and even then, I would still point out that the trend is based on a small sample. This means you need more than fifty fights under your belt just to make a single statement from experience about how often they go to the ground. You will need even more fights for answering questions about low-probability events, such as how often your opponent will have pepper spray in his pocket. If 1 percent of the type of opponents you encounter will have pepper spray, you might get into one hundred fights before you even have a single pepper spray experience. The number of fights grows for each unknown factor an experienced fighter needs to be prepared for, especially for conditional statements, such as, "If a fight does go to the ground, how often will friends or bystanders get involved?" Given the number of possible scenarios, possible opponents, possible techniques both you and your opponents could use, and all the different ways each technique can possibly go right or wrong, even if the number of fights you need to develop a solid expertise is fewer than sixty thousand, it is still far beyond what any human could ever endure in one lifetime.

In his book *Meditations on Violence: A Comparison of Martial Arts Training & Real World Violence*, Sergeant Rory Miller, a martial artist and a veteran corrections officer with a much-larger-than-average set of personal violent experiences, talks about how he has needed to defend himself from someone with a knife on five separate occasions. This number is much higher than most civilians would ever expect to encounter, but it is still grossly insufficient to start to develop any real expertise. He even goes as far as to say all five of his encounters would have been considered special cases that didn't really count when portraying a "typical" encounter for training purposes. Chances are if you ever need to defend yourself from a knife, your encounter will also be a special case that doesn't count. There are just too many variables at play to learn anything meaningful from small numbers.

If you want to try to learn from the experiences of others, there are some sources of aggregate data, such as police reports, but we learned in chapter 8 these sources carry misleading biases. The experiences of law enforcement officers and military personnel are not the same types of experiences civilians encounter, and any videos of real fights you find online will be biased toward sensationalism. The only statistically meaningful way to learn about violence would be to conduct large-scale surveys designed to answer one very specific question at a time. The problem with this is that even if you can learn from aggregate experiences, violence and fighting are moving targets. Criminal tactics and scenarios can come and go like fashions and change with technology, and it can be nearly impossible to keep such a large effort up to date.

You don't need to be an expert if you can fight like a physicist.

Even though your training will bear little resemblance to the ring or the streets, and even though it is impossible for your body to endure the tens of thousands of fights it would take to become a true fighting expert, this does not mean studying martial arts is pointless. It just means you need to train for the unknown. There are some academic disciplines, like engineering, where the material you study and the problems you solve are very similar to how it is applied in real life. People who pursue careers in these disciplines tend to be efficient and incredibly accurate (and well paid), but they are not well adapted to unexplored territory. Physicists, on the other hand, train specifically for the unknown. Of course, in familiar territory, physicists tend to be slower and sloppier than engineers, but when it comes to making new discoveries, developing new insights, and diving headfirst into topics nobody has ever studied before, no one is better equipped for the challenge than a physicist. For this reason, I propose that if you take the same approach to studying martial arts that a physics student takes when studying physics, you will have the best chance of applying your training experience to both the street and the ring.

There are many subtle differences between the educational approaches in fields like physics and engineering, and not all of them are meaningful, so instead of attempting to capture them all, I will pick four points you can try to incorporate into your training to better prepare yourself for the unknown.

Be a skeptic. Respect your instructors, but also remember they are experts in the subject of martial arts training, not fighting. Even if they are former champions themselves, the best they can do is offer you a glimpse into what happened to work for them. Keep your ears open for potential garbage at all times. Some of the most common red flags for garbage are speaking in absolutes ("This kick will always knock him out") and making untestable claims ("This kick will break the knee," or "This strike will kill your opponent"). The truth is you have no good way of knowing what will happen as a result of most of your techniques. Replace untested assumptions with uncertainty, and learn to embrace that uncertainty.

Ask why. At the most basic level, you want to ask "why" to make sure you understand the technique. Ask, "Why do we tuck our thumb in for this technique?" or "Why do we turn our foot for this kick?" The more you understand the "why" behind a rule, the better you will understand when it is OK to break it. Go deeper with your questions and ask about choices. Ask, "Why do we use a knife hand to strike the neck instead of a straight punch?" Go even deeper and ask about strategy with questions such as, "Why do we kick the leg?" Ultimately, ask about goals, such as, "What are we trying to accomplish by punching our opponent?" No instructor could ever answer every question you ask, and different instructors may have different answers to the same question, so don't be disappointed if they don't always have a good answer, but don't forget to be skeptical as you listen either.

Break everything. Every technique you learn, every strategy you employ, every weapon you use, and every piece of safety gear you wear, you should try to break. Find out what the limits are on your own terms, when you have time to soak it all in, instead of when you need your mind focused on your opponent. If you learned how to block a punch, have a friend throw punches harder and harder until one either flies through the block or hurts your arm. See what happens when you block too close or too far away. Does it also work on kicks? Try out various incoming punch angles. Take each technique to multiple extremes, and make a mental note of not only how far you can take it, but also the way it breaks down when you get there.

Get it wrong on purpose. Make mistakes when you practice a technique with a partner and make mistakes when you spar. Mistakes are learning opportunities, and you won't get enough of them if you are always flawless in class. Get sloppy and watch what happens. Overcommit, drop your hands, or use a narrow base on the mat. Zone out or let yourself get distracted for a moment and see what it takes to recover. Get used to making mistakes and dealing with the repercussions.

These are just a few examples, but hopefully it is enough to get you started. You can take it in whatever direction you want from here. Now put the book down and go train.

GLOSSARY

Abbott, David "Tank." A heavyweight mixed martial artist known for his ferocious performances and unsportsmanlike conduct in the early days of the UFC. Abbott wore fingerless gloves to protect his hands before gloves were required by MMA rules.

acupuncture. A pseudoscientific healing method where a practitioner places needles subdermally at special points on meridians to positively affect a patient's qi.

angular momentum. The rotational equivalent of momentum, defined as the cross product of the moment of inertia and the angular velocity.

angular velocity. The rate at which an object rotates in a particular direction, defined as the change in angle divided by the change in time.

axon. A long nerve fiber extending from one neuron to other neurons, used to transmit information.

boxing. A Western combat sport and Olympic sport where athletes compete with closed-fist strikes only. Clinch fighting, grappling, throws, and kicks are not allowed. Modern boxers also wear large gloves and wrap their hands.

boxing gloves. Large padded gloves with covered fingers, used in combination with hand wraps for combat sports.

Brazilian jiu-jitsu. A Brazilian martial art derived from judo, focusing primarily on grappling and submissions. Developed and popularized by the Gracie family.

center of mass. A single point defined as the weighted average position of all the small components that make up an object. An object will balance whenever it is supported directly underneath its center of mass.

center of rotation. The point an object rotates around. If an object's motion is not constrained in any way, the center of rotation will be located at the center of mass.

chi sao drills. A two-person drill where one or both hands are kept in contact with the opponent's hands, and slight variations in pressure indicate either an opportunity to attack or a need to defend.

Chinese herbal treatments. Pseudoscientific healing methods where traditional herbs are ingested in an attempt to induce a positive influence on a person's qi.

chronic traumatic encephalopathy (CTE). A neurodegenerative disorder caused by repeated blows to the head. Commonly found in professional fighters, football players, and athletes in other contact sports.

circumference. The distance of the path around a circle.

clinch fighting. Fighting at close range where combatants can grab each other but still remain standing.

dan tian. Part of the set of pseudoscientific beliefs associated with qi. Believed to be the source of qi in the body. Located near your center of mass, just below the belly button.

dao sword. A Chinese saber, curved and bladed on only one side.

diameter. The full width of a circle. The diameter can be found by measuring the length of a straight line that connects two opposite points on a circle and passes through the circle's center.

diffuse axonal injury (DAI). A type of brain injury where axons throughout the brain are damaged as a result of sheer forces during rapid rotational acceleration.

Dog Brothers. A community of stick fighters well known for holding "gatherings" where combatants test their skills with full contact and minimal protective gear.

effective mass. An estimated property of a strike based on the observed force in the target, where the complicated contributions from an athlete's muscles and technique are simplified into a percentage of the athlete's body mass that can be considered "behind" the strike.

Einstein, Albert. A well-known German-American twentieth-century theoretical physicist. Einstein developed the theory of relativity, won a Nobel Prize for his work on the photoelectric effect, and earned a reputation as one of the greatest scientific minds of all time.

energy. A scalar physical quantity representing an amount of work that can be performed moving an object. Energy can change into many forms, such as light, heat, sound, motion, or structural damage, but energy cannot be created or destroyed.

eskrima. A Filipino martial art, also called kali or arnis, focusing on stick and blade techniques.

eskrima stick. A stick used for fighting in eskrima and other martial arts styles. Typically made from rattan and cut to arm's length.

Feynman, Richard. A twentieth-century American theoretical physicist who received the Nobel Prize in 1965 for his contributions to quantum electrodynamics.

force. An interaction with the ability to cause specific directional changes to the momentum of an object over time. In the context of a fight, the most relevant forces are the force of gravity and the forces generated by muscles in the human body. The colloquial definition of "force" or "power" used to describe strikes in martial arts is not the same as the definition used in physics.

fulcrum. The point around which a lever rotates.

gi. A martial arts uniform.

gongfu. A general term used to describe a number of different Chinese martial art styles.

Gracie, Royce. A Brazilian mixed martial artist and champion of the first Ultimate Fighting Championship tournament. Son of the cofounder of Brazilian jiu-jitsu, Helio Gracie.

grandmaster. An expert instructor of high degree within a martial arts style.

grappling. The art of fighting at the closest possible range, where both combatants are in close contact on the ground. Typically excludes striking techniques.

gravity. An attractive force between any two objects, but in this book we focus on the attraction between the Earth and person-sized objects near the surface of the Earth. In this regime, gravity provides a constant downward acceleration of 32 feet per second squared (9.8 m/s^2).

hapkido. A Korean martial art that combines "hard" elements, such as punches and kicks, with "soft" elements, such as throws, pressure points, and joint manipulation.

haymaker. A punch used primarily by untrained fighters where the elbow stays extended and the arm rotates at the shoulder.

jeet kune do. A modern martial art developed by Bruce Lee, focusing on self-defense. Influenced by a number of different styles, including wing chun, boxing, and fencing.

juji gatame. The classic grappling arm bar, commonly used as a submission in judo, Brazilian jiu-jitsu, and mixed martial arts competitions, where the arm is hyperextended at the elbow.

judo. A Japanese martial art and Olympic sport, featuring throws, grappling, and submissions.

karate. A Japanese martial art focusing on hard strikes with the hands and feet. Karate is taught both as a sport and a method of self-defense.

kendo. A Japanese combat sport where practitioners wear body armor and wield practice swords made from bamboo.

kenpo. An American martial art with mixed Japanese and Chinese origins, focusing on self-defense techniques. Kenpo uses hard strikes as well as submissions and joint manipulation.

kickboxing. A combat sport that allows strikes with hands and feet. Participants typically wear hand wraps and boxing gloves.

lever. A simple tool made from a rigid arm rotating around a fulcrum. Allows you to turn a small force at a long distance from the fulcrum into a large force at a short distance from the fulcrum, and vice versa.

mass. A physical property of an object that determines the force required to set it in motion at a given velocity. On the surface of the Earth, the mass of an object is proportional to the weight of that object.

meridian. Part of the set of pseudoscientific beliefs associated with qi. Believed to be a mystic channel for qi in the body.

mixed martial arts (MMA). A modern combat sport that allows for a wide range of striking, grappling, and submission techniques.

mixed martial arts gloves. Small padded gloves with open fingers, used in combination with hand wraps for mixed martial arts events.

moment of inertia. The rotational equivalent of mass, defined as the mass times the distance from the center of rotation squared, summed up for each small component of an object.

momentum. A property of an object defined as the product of mass and velocity. Momentum can be transferred from one object to another, but only external forces can change the total momentum of a system.

muay boran. A Thai martial art and combat sport practiced before the introduction of muay Thai.

muay Thai. A Thai combat sport that allows strikes with hands, feet, knees, and elbows. Includes both striking and clinch fighting.

National Crime Victimization Survey (NCVS). A biannual survey conducted in the United States by the Bureau of Justice Statistics for the purpose of studying crime victimization without the selection biases found in police reports and other sources.

National Operating Committee on Standards for Athletic Equipment (NOCSAE). A nonprofit organization responsible for providing safety standards for helmets used in football and other sports. NOCSAE uses criteria that keep athletes safe from skull fractures, but not concussions or CTE.

nociceptors. Sensory neuron receptors responsible for detecting potentially damaging stimuli and sending signals to the brain. The brain may then interpret the signals as pain.

peak force. The highest momentary value measured by a force meter during an impact such as a punch or a kick. Peak force is a common metric, but it is generally unreliable and insufficient when used for measuring strikes.

physics. A branch of science without a strict topical definition, focusing on uncovering the natural structures of our universe with mathematical and experimental tool sets. Introductory physics classes tend to focus on Newtonian mechanics, electricity, and magnetism.

pi. The ratio of the circumference of a circle to its diameter, often approximated as 3.14. Pi is a fundamental constant of the universe.

pseudoscience. A claim or belief that bears some superficial resemblance to scientific claims but is not grounded in science.

qi. A pseudoscientific concept typically translated as a sort of "life energy." Qi is fundamentally entangled within a much larger set of mystic beliefs.

qigong. A set of practices, including low-impact exercise, meditation, and abdominal breathing, intended to provide health benefits. Qigong is taught with an emphasis on the concept of qi.

Reiki. A Japanese pseudoscientific energy therapy, similar to therapeutic touch, where a trained practitioner places hands on or near a patient and allegedly transfers qi in order to heal him or her.

Queensbury rules. A set of rules for boxing matches, published by the Marques of Queensbury in 1867. These rules were the first to require the use of boxing gloves.

radius. The distance from any point on a circle to the center of the circle.

sambo. A Russian martial art combining elements from judo and traditional wrestling.

skepticism. A scientific approach to the acquisition of knowledge, where no authority is considered infallible and information is checked for consistency or verified externally whenever possible. Skepticism also includes the acceptance of uncertainty for unverifiable claims.

Sullivan, John L. An American pugilist and world bareknuckle boxing champion from 1882 to 1892. Also known as the "Boston Strong Boy."

taekwondo. A Korean martial art and Olympic sport allowing strikes with hands and feet, but with a strong emphasis on kicking.

taiji. A Chinese martial art often taught as a low-impact exercise rather than a method of self-defense. Explanations of taiji techniques are traditionally rooted in the concept of qi.

therapeutic touch. A pseudoscientific energy healing method invented in the 1970s by a nurse and a mystic author. Debunked in the 1990s when practitioners were tested and could not sense the presence or absence of a human hand.

Ultimate Fighting Championship (UFC). The most popular mixed martial arts promotion today. Originally promoted as a single tournament pitting experts from different fighting styles against each other.

vale tudo. A traditional Brazilian martial arts competition with very limited rules.

velocity. A measure of how fast an object is moving, coupled with the direction in which the object is traveling.

wedge. A simple tool shaped like a triangle with one short side and two long sides. When an outside force is applied to the short side of a wedge, the force is split in two and redirected perpendicular to the two long sides.

wing chun. A Chinese martial art with a square-shoulder stance, focusing on self-defense using rapid, close-range strikes.

wrestling. An Olympic combat sport featuring grappling and takedown techniques. Many mixed martial arts champions come from a strong wrestling background.

wushu. A modern exhibition sport based on empty-hand and weapon forms from traditional Chinese martial arts. Wushu is often used for choreographing fight scenes in movies and on television.

WORKS CITED

Baker, A. (2007, December 9). A hail of bullets, a heap of uncertainty. *The New York Times*.

Bartsch, A., Benzel, E., Miele, V., & Prakash, V. (2012). Impact test comparisons of 20th and 21st century American football helmets: Laboratory investigation. *Journal of Neurosurgery, 116* (1), 222–233.

Beaman, V., Annest, J. L., Mercy, J. A., Kresnow, M. J., & Pollock, D. A. (2000). Lethality of firearm-related injuries in the United States population. *Annals of Emergency Medicine, 35* (3), 258–266.

Blair, J. P., Pollock, J., Montague, D., Nichols, T., Curnutt, J., & Burns, D. (2011). Reasonableness and reaction time. *Police Quarterly, 14* (4), 323–343.

Block, R. (1981). Victim-offender dynamics in violent crime. *Journal of Criminal Law and Criminology*, 743–761.

Boatman, R. H. (2005). *Living with the 1911: A fresh look at the fighting gun*. Boulder, CO: Paladin Press.

Cao, H., Liu, J., & Lewith, G. T. (2010). Traditional Chinese medicine for treatment of fibromyalgia: A systematic review of randomized controlled trials. *The Journal of Alternative and Complementary Medicine, 16* (4), 397–409.

Chen, J. H., Liu, C., You, L., & Simmons, C. A. (2010). Boning up on Wolff's law: Mechanical regulation of the cells that make and maintain bone. *Journal of Biomechanics, 43* (1), 108–118.

Colquhoun, D., & Novella, S. P. (2013). Acupuncture is theatrical placebo. *Anesthesia & Analgesia, 116* (6), 1360–1363.

Cosyns, J. P. (2003). Aristolochic acid and 'Chinese herbs nephropathy': A review of the evidence to date. *Drug Safety, 26* (1), 33–48.

Crandall, M., Sharp, D., Unger, E., Straus, D., Brasel, K., Hsia, R., et al. (2013). Trauma deserts: Distance from a trauma center, transport times, and mortality from gunshot wounds in Chicago. *American Journal of Public Health, 103* (6), 1103–1109.

Eiband, A. M. (1959). Human tolerance to rapidly applied accelerations: A summary of the literature. *NASA* (19980228043).

Feld, M. S., McNair, R. E., & Wilk, S. R. (1979). The physics of karate. *Scientific American, 240* (4), 150–158.

Fiedler, M. D., Jones, L. M., Miller, S. F., & Finley, R. K. (1986). A correlation of response time and results of abdominal gunshot wounds. *Archives of Surgery, 121* (8), 902–904.

Gadd, C. (1966). Use of a weighted-impulse criterion for estimating injury hazard. *Proceedings, 10th Stapp Car Crash Conf.*, 164–174.

Gladwell, M. (2008). *Outliers: The story of success.*

Gotsch, K. E., Annest, J. L., Mercy, J. A., & Ryan, G. W. (2001). Surveillance for fatal and nonfatal firearm-related injuries—United States, 1993–1998. *MMWR Morbity and Mortality Weekly Report, 50*, 1–32.

Gurdjian, E. S., Roberts, V. L., & Thomas, L. M. (1966). Tolerance curves of acceleration and intracranial pressure and protective index in experimental head injury. *Journal of Trauma-Injury, Infection, and Critical Care, 6* (5), 600–604.

Gwin, J. T., Chu, J. J., Diamond, S. G., Halstead, P. D., Crisco, J. J., & Greenwald, R. M. (2010). An investigation of the NOCSAE linear impactor test method based on in vivo measures of head impact acceleration in American football. *Journal of Biomechanical Engineering, 132* (1), 011006.

Isaacson, W. (2011). *Steve Jobs.* New York: Simon & Schuster.

Johnson, V. E., Stewart, W., & Smith, D. H. (2013). Axonal pathology in traumatic brain injury. *Experimental Neurology, 246*, 35–43.

King, A. I., Yang, K. H., Zhang, L., Hardy, W., & Viano, D. C. (2003). Is head injury caused by linear or angular acceleration? *In IRCOBI conference*, 1–12.

Kosinski, R. J. (2013). *A Literature Review on Reaction Time.* (Clemson University) Retrieved from http://biae.clemson.edu/bpc/bp/lab/110/reaction.htm

Lee, M. S., Oh, B., & Ernst, E. (2011). Qigong for healthcare: An overview of systematic reviews. *JRSM Short Reports, 2* (2), 7.

Lee, M. S., Pittler, M. H., & Ernst, E. (2008). Effects of Reiki in clinical practice: A systematic review of randomised clinical trials. *International Journal of Clinical Practice, 62* (6), 947–954.

Lee, M. S., Pittler, M. H., & Ernst, E. (2009). Internal qigong for pain conditions: A systematic review. *The Journal of Pain, 10* (11), 1121–1127.

Liu, X., Zhang, M., He, L., Li, Y. P., & Kang, Y. K. (2006). Chinese herbs combined with Western medicine for severe acute respiratory syndrome (SARS). *Cochrane Database Syst Rev*, 1.

Ma, B. G. (2011). Epidemiology, quality and reporting characteristics of systematic reviews of traditional Chinese medicine interventions published in Chinese journals. *PLoS One, 6* (5), e20185.

Madsen, M. V., Gøtzsche, P. C., & Hróbjartsson, A. (2009). Acupuncture treatment for pain: Systematic review of randomised clinical trials with acupuncture, placebo acupuncture, and no acupuncture groups. *BMJ, 338*.

Martland, H. S. (1928). Punch drunk. *The Journal of the American Medical Association, 91*, 1103–1107.

Mayer, A. R., Ling, J., Mannell, M. V., Gasparovic, C., Phillips, J. P., Doezema, D., et al. (2010). A prospective diffusion tensor imaging study in mild traumatic brain injury. *Neurology, 74* (8), 643–650.

McKee, A. C., Cantu, R. C., Nowinski, C. J., Hedley-Whyte, E. T., Gavett, B. E., Budson, A. E., et al. (2009). Chronic traumatic encephalopathy in athletes: Progressive tauopathy following repetitive head injury. *Journal of Neuropathology and Experimental Neurology, 68* (7), 709.

Meany, D. F., Smith, D. H., Shreiber, D. I., Bain, A. C., Miller, R. T., Ross, D. T., et al. (1995). Biomechanical analysis of experimental diffuse axonal injury. *Journal of Neurotrauma, 12* (4), 689–694.

Millspaugh, J. A. (1937). Dementia pugilistica. *US Naval Med Bull, 35,* 297–303.

Moffet, H. H. (2009). Sham acupuncture may be as efficacious as true acupuncture: A systematic review of clinical trials. *The Journal of Alternative and Complementary Medicine, 15* (3), 213–216.

New York City Police Department. (2013). *2012 Annual Firearms Discharge Report.* New York: NYPD.

O'Driscoll, S. W., Horii, E., Ness, R., Cahalan, T. D., Richards, R. R., & An, K. N. (1992). The relationship between wrist position, grasp size, and grip strength. *The Journal of Hand Surgery, 17* (1), 169–177.

Omalu, B. I., DeKosky, S. T., Minster, R. L., Kamboh, M. I., Hamilton, R. L., & Wecht, C. H. (2005). Chronic traumatic encephalopathy in a National Football League player. *Neurosurgery, 57* (1), 128–134.

Park, J. E., Hong, S., Lee, M., Park, T., Kang, K., Jung, H., et al. (2013). Randomized, controlled trial of qigong for treatment of prehypertension and mild essential hypertension. *Alternative Therapies in Health and Medicine, 20* (4), 21–30.

Park, J., White, A., Stevinson, C., Ernst, E., & James, M. (2002). Validating a new non-penetrating sham acupuncture device: Two randomised controlled trials. *Acupuncture in Medicine, 20* (4), 168–174.

Perkins, C. (2003). *Weapon Use and Violent Crime.* US Department of Justice, Office of Justice Programs, Bureau of Justice Statistics.

Reyssat, E., Tallinen, T., Le Merrer, M., & Mahadevan, L. (2012). Slicing softly with shear. *Physical Review Letters, 109* (24), 244301.

Rosa, L., Rosa, E., Sarner, L., & Barrett, S. (1998). A close look at therapeutic touch. *JAMA, 279* (13), 1005–1010.

Roush, G. C. (2010). *Finding cadaveric human head masses and center of gravity: A comparison of direct measurement to 3D modeling* (Unpublished master's thesis). Wright State University, Dayton, Ohio.

Shang, A., Huwiler, K., Nartey, L., Jüni, P., & Egger, M. (2007). Placebo-controlled trials of Chinese herbal medicine and conventional medicine—comparative study. *International Journal of Epidemiology, 36* (5), 1086–1092.

Singh, S., & Ernst, E. M. (2008). *Trick or treatment: The undeniable facts about alternative medicine.* London: WW Norton & Company.

Small, G. W., Kepe, V., Siddarth, P., Ercoli, L. M., Merrill, D. A., Donoghue, N., et al. (2013). PET scanning of brain tau in retired national football league players: Preliminary findings. *The American Journal of Geriatric Psychiatry, 21* (2), 138–144.

Smith, D. H., & Meaney, D. F. (2000). Axonal damage in traumatic brain injury. *The Neuroscientist, 6* (6), 483–495.

Smith, D. H., Nonaka, M., Miller, R., Leoni, M., Chen, X. H., Alsop, D., et al. (2000). Immediate coma following inertial brain injury dependent on axonal damage in the brainstem. *Journal of Neurosurgery, 93* (2), 315–322.

Takhounts, E. G., Ridella, S. A., Hasija, V., Tannous, R. E., Campbell, J. Q., Malone, D., et al. (2008). Investigation of traumatic brain injuries using the next generation of simulated injury monitor (SIMon) finite element head model. *Stapp Car Crash J, 52,* 1–31.

Tark, J., & Kleck, G. (2004). Resisting crime: The effects of victim action on the outcomes of crimes. *Criminology, 42* (4), 861–910.

Thompson, M. P., Simon, T. R., Saltzman, L. E., & Mercy, J. A. (1999). Epidemiology of injuries among women after physical assaults: The role of self-protective behaviors. *American Journal of Epidemiology, 150* (3), 235–244.

Van Agtmael, M. A., Eggelte, T. A., & van Boxtel, C. J. (1999). Artemisinin drugs in the treatment of malaria: From medicinal herb to registered medication. *Trends in Pharmacological Sciences, 20* (5), 199–205.

VanderVaart, S., Gijsen, V. M., de Wildt, S. N., & Koren, G. (2009). A systematic review of the therapeutic effects of Reiki. *The Journal of Alternative and Complementary Medicine, 15* (11), 1157–1169.

Versace, J. (1971). A review of severity of index. *Proceedings, 15th Stapp Car Crash Conf.,* SAE Paper No. 710881.

Verschueren, S. M., Bogaerts, A., Delecluse, C., Claessens, A. L., Haentjens, P., Vanderschueren, D., et al. (2011). The effects of whole-body vibration training and vitamin D supplementation on muscle strength, muscle mass, and bone density in institutionalized elderly women: A 6-month randomized, controlled trial. *Journal of Bone and Mineral Research, 26* (1), 42–49.

Vickers, A. J., Cronin, A. M., Maschino, A. C., Lewith, G., MacPherson, H., Foster, N. E., et al. (2012). Acupuncture for chronic pain: Individual patient data meta-analysis. *Archives of Internal Medicine, 172* (19), 1444–1453.

Walker, J. (2010). *Boiling and the Leidenfrost effect.*

Walker, L. B., Harris, E. H., & Pontius, U. R. (1973). Mass, volume, center of mass and mass moment of inertia of head and head and neck of the human body (Doctoral dissertation). Retrieved from Defense Technical Information Center (AD0762581).

Wang, Y. Y., Li, X. X., Liu, J. P., Luo, H., Ma, L. X., & Alraek, T. (2014). Traditional Chinese medicine for chronic fatigue syndrome: A systematic review of randomized clinical trials. *Complementary therapies in medicine, 22* (4), 826–833.

Webb, E. W. (1999). A comparison of fatal with non-fatal knife injuries in Edinburgh. *Forensic science international, 99* (3), 179–187.

Willey, D. (2010). Fire-walking. *Physics Education, 45* (5), 487.

Yang, J.-M. (1997). *The root of Chinese qigong.* Wolfeboro, NH: YMAA Publication Center.

INDEX

ABOUT THE AUTHOR

JASON THALKEN has a PhD in computational condensed matter physics from the University of Southern California, and bachelor's degrees in physics, mathematics, and philosophy from the University of Texas. He is the inventor on eight patent applications for data science and

modeling in the financial services industry, and one patent application for protecting the brain from trauma in such sports as boxing, MMA, and football. Jason has studied and competed in numerous martial arts styles since 1995 and has a black belt in hapkido under Grandmaster Ho Jin Song.

Jason grew up deep in the woods of Massachusetts, where he cultivated an early love of the natural world and had already decided to become a scientist by the time he was seven. After moving to the suburbs of Dallas, he started taking taekwondo, and he fell in love with the complex chaos of fighting when he broke his foot at his very first competition.

Once, when Jason was still an undergraduate competing on the University of Texas judo team, he ended up a half pound too heavy at the weigh-ins, and was instructed to try again in one hour. The entire UT judo team immediately stripped down to their underwear, gave Jason their clothes, and cheered him on as he ran laps around the parking lot, did jumping jacks, chewed gum, and spat, all while stuffed inside a hot, restrictive cocoon of layered shirts and pants. At the end of the hour, he had lost a half pound of spit and sweat, thanks to the support of his mostly naked cheerleaders.

Jason Thalken has spent the last fifteen years in Austin, Los Angeles, and New York City, and currently resides in Seattle, Washington, with his family.

BOOKS FROM YMAA

101 REFLECTIONS ON TAI CHI CHUAN
108 INSIGHTS INTO TAI CHI CHUAN
A WOMAN'S QIGONG GUIDE
ADVANCING IN TAE KWON DO
ANALYSIS OF SHAOLIN CHIN NA 2ND ED
ANCIENT CHINESE WEAPONS
ART AND SCIENCE OF STAFF FIGHTING
THE ART AND SCIENCE OF SELF-DEFENSE
ART AND SCIENCE OF STICK FIGHTING
ART OF HOJO UNDO
ARTHRITIS RELIEF, 3D ED.
BACK PAIN RELIEF, 2ND ED.
BAGUAZHANG, 2ND ED.
BRAIN FITNESS
CHIN NA IN GROUND FIGHTING
CHINESE FAST WRESTLING
CHINESE FITNESS
CHINESE TUI NA MASSAGE
COMPLETE MARTIAL ARTIST
COMPREHENSIVE APPLICATIONS OF SHAOLIN CHIN NA
CONFLICT COMMUNICATION
DAO DE JING: A QIGONG INTERPRETATION
DAO IN ACTION
DEFENSIVE TACTICS
DIRTY GROUND
DR. WU'S HEAD MASSAGE
ESSENCE OF SHAOLIN WHITE CRANE
EXPLORING TAI CHI
FACING VIOLENCE
FIGHT LIKE A PHYSICIST
THE FIGHTER'S BODY
FIGHTER'S FACT BOOK 1&2
FIGHTING ARTS
FIGHTING THE PAIN RESISTANT ATTACKER
FIRST DEFENSE
FORCE DECISIONS: A CITIZENS GUIDE
INSIDE TAI CHI
JUDO ADVANTAGE
JUJI GATAME ENCYCLOPEDIA
KARATE SCIENCE
KATA AND THE TRANSMISSION OF KNOWLEDGE
KRAV MAGA COMBATIVES
KRAV MAGA FUNDAMENTAL STRATEGIES
KRAV MAGA PROFESSIONAL TACTICS
KRAV MAGA WEAPON DEFENSES
LITTLE BLACK BOOK OF VIOLENCE
LIUHEBAFA FIVE CHARACTER SECRETS
MARTIAL ARTS OF VIETNAM
MARTIAL ARTS INSTRUCTION
MARTIAL WAY AND ITS VIRTUES
MEDITATIONS ON VIOLENCE
MERIDIAN QIGONG EXERCISES
MINDFUL EXERCISE
MIND INSIDE TAI CHI
MIND INSIDE YANG STYLE TAI CHI CHUAN
NATURAL HEALING WITH QIGONG
NORTHERN SHAOLIN SWORD, 2ND ED.
OKINAWA'S COMPLETE KARATE SYSTEM: ISSHIN RYU
PRINCIPLES OF TRADITIONAL CHINESE MEDICINE
PROTECTOR ETHIC
QIGONG FOR HEALTH & MARTIAL ARTS 2ND ED.
QIGONG FOR TREATING COMMON AILMENTS

QIGONG MASSAGE
QIGONG MEDITATION: EMBRYONIC BREATHING
QIGONG GRAND CIRCULATION
QIGONG MEDITATION: SMALL CIRCULATION
QIGONG, THE SECRET OF YOUTH: DA MO'S CLASSICS
REDEMPTION
ROOT OF CHINESE QIGONG, 2ND ED.
SAMBO ENCYCLOPEDIA
SCALING FORCE
SELF-DEFENSE FOR WOMEN
SHIN GI TAI: KARATE TRAINING
SIMPLE CHINESE MEDICINE
SIMPLE QIGONG EXERCISES FOR HEALTH, 3RD ED.
SIMPLIFIED TAI CHI CHUAN, 2ND ED.
SOLO TRAINING 1&2
SPOTTING DANGER BEFORE IT SPOTS YOU
SPOTTING DANGER BEFORE IT SPOTS YOUR KIDS
SPOTTING DANGER BEFORE IT SPOTS YOUR TEENS
SUMO FOR MIXED MARTIAL ARTS
SUNRISE TAI CHI
SURVIVING ARMED ASSAULTS
TAE KWON DO: THE KOREAN MARTIAL ART
TAEKWONDO BLACK BELT POOMSAE
TAEKWONDO: A PATH TO EXCELLENCE
TAEKWONDO: ANCIENT WISDOM
TAEKWONDO: DEFENSE AGAINST WEAPONS
TAEKWONDO: SPIRIT AND PRACTICE
TAI CHI BALL QIGONG: FOR HEALTH AND MARTIAL ARTS
TAI CHI BALL WORKOUT FOR BEGINNERS
THE TAI CHI BOOK
TAI CHI CHIN NA, 2ND ED.
TAI CHI CHUAN CLASSICAL YANG STYLE, 2ND ED.
TAI CHI CHUAN MARTIAL POWER, 3RD ED.
TAI CHI CONCEPTS AND EXPERIMENTS
TAI CHI CONNECTIONS
TAI CHI DYNAMICS
TAI CHI FOR DEPRESSION
TAI CHI IN 10 WEEKS
TAI CHI PUSH HANDS
TAI CHI QIGONG, 3RD ED.
TAI CHI SECRETS OF THE ANCIENT MASTERS
TAI CHI SECRETS OF THE WU & LI STYLES
TAI CHI SECRETS OF THE WU STYLE
TAI CHI SECRETS OF THE YANG STYLE
TAI CHI SWORD: CLASSICAL YANG STYLE, 2ND ED.
TAI CHI SWORD FOR BEGINNERS
TAI CHI WALKING
TAIJIQUAN THEORY OF DR. YANG, JWING-MING
FIGHTING ARTS
TRADITIONAL CHINESE HEALTH SECRETS
TRADITIONAL TAEKWONDO
TRAINING FOR SUDDEN VIOLENCE
TRIANGLE HOLD ENCYCLOPEDIA
TRUE WELLNESS SERIES (MIND, HEART, GUT)
WARRIOR'S MANIFESTO
WAY OF KATA
WAY OF SANCHIN KATA
WAY TO BLACK BELT
WESTERN HERBS FOR MARTIAL ARTISTS
WILD GOOSE QIGONG
WINNING FIGHTS
XINGYIQUAN

AND MANY MORE . . .

VIDEOS FROM YMAA

AND MANY MORE . . .

more products available from . . .
YMAA Publication Center, Inc. 楊氏東方文化出版中心
1-800-669-8892 • info@ymaa.com • www.ymaa.com